English

Brush Up

Berlitz Languages, Inc.
Princeton, NJ
USA

Copyright© 1987 Berlitz Languages, Inc.

All rights reserved. No part of this book may be reproduced or transmitted in any form or by any means, electronic or mechanical, including photocopying, recording or by any information storage and retrieval system without permission in writing from the Publisher.

Berlitz Languages, Inc. and its affiliates are the sole proprietors of the name Berlitz in connection with language instruction, language textbooks, language tapes and cassettes, and language schools throughout the world. The use of the name Berlitz in such connection is hereby specifically prohibited unless formally authorized by contract with Berlitz. The purchase or repurchase of this book or any other Berlitz publication in no way entitles the purchaser or any other person to the use of the name Berlitz in connection with the teaching of languages.

Berlitz Trademark Reg. U.S. Patent Office and other countries
Marca Registrada

Cover photo
Images © PhotoDisc, Inc. 1994

ISBN 2-8315-2160-2

Illustrations
Jim Woodend

15th Printing – August 1997
Printed in Swizerland by Presses Centrales Lausanne SA

For use exclusively in connection with Berlitz classroom instruction

Berlitz Languages, Inc.
400 Alexander Park
Princeton, NJ
USA

TABLE OF CONTENTS

Introduction vii

Chapter 1

Dialog	**Do You Two Know Each Other?**	1
Culture Tip	**Friends at First Sight**	2
Exercise 1	Simple Present vs. Present Progressive	3
Exercise 2	Adverbs of Frequency	4
Text	**Churchill Meets Churchill**	5
Exercise 3	Indirect Object Pronouns	6
Exercise 4	**Still • anymore**	7

Chapter 2

Dialog	**When Can We Get Together?**	9
Culture Tip	**Let's Grab a Bite**	10
Exercise 5	**Can • should • may • must**	11
Exercise 6	Expressing Probability	12
Text	**Psycho-Sell: Are You Immune?**	13
Exercise 7	**Some • any • a lot • no • much • many • a few • a little**	14
Exercise 8	**Want to • have to • like to**	15

Chapter 3

Dialog	**Back Already?**	17
Culture Tip	**How Much Vacation?**	18
Exercise 9	The Simple Past	19
Exercise 10	Short Answers with *too* and *either*	20
Text	**James Macie's Will**	21
Exercise 11	Possessive Adjectives and Pronouns	22
Exercise 12	Simple Present vs. Simple Past	23

Chapter 4

Dialog	**I'd Like to Speak to the Manager**	25

Culture Tip	Stick to Your Guns	26
Exercise 13	The Present Perfect	27
Exercise 14	Yet • already • for • since	28
Text	California — Fantasyland	29
Exercise 15	Contrasting Tenses	30
Exercise 16	Comparatives • Superlatives	31

Chapter 5

Dialog	What's Going on Out There?	33
Culture Tip	Combining Business with Pleasure	34
Exercise 17	Future Time	35
Exercise 18	Combining Sentences	36
Text	Timing Is Everything!	37
Exercise 19	Too • enough • too much • too many	38
Exercise 20	Gerunds after Prepositions	39

Chapter 6

Dialog	I'll Take It!	41
Culture Tip	Cash or Charge?	42
Exercise 21	The Past Progressive	43
Exercise 22	Present Perfect Progressive	44
Text	See You at the Mall!	45
Exercise 23	Question Clauses	46
Exercise 24	More / less / fewer ... than • as much / as many ... as	47

Chapter 7

Dialog	Where Is That Waiter?	49
Culture Tip	Trends in Restaurants	50
Exercise 25	Passive Voice	51
Exercise 26	Tag Questions	52
Text	To Tip or Not to Tip?	53
Exercise 27	Active vs. Passive Voice	54
Exercise 28	Participles as Adjectives	55

Chapter 8

Dialog	**What's the Trouble?**	57
Culture Tip	**The Changing Role of Women**	58
Exercise 29	Causatives	59
Exercise 30	Reflexive Pronouns • *each other*	60
Text	**Rolls Royce Gets Rolling**	61
Exercise 31	Passive with Modals	62
Exercise 32	Separable Phrasal Verbs	63

Chapter 9

Dialog	**You Really Had Quite a Day!**	65
Culture Tip	**Knock on Wood**	66
Exercise 33	The Past Perfect	67
Exercise 34	Contrasting Tenses	68
Text	**Better Safe Than Sorry**	69
Exercise 35	Conjunctions	70
Exercise 36	Word Families	71

Chapter 10

Dialog	**An Invitation**	73
Culture Tip	**You're Invited**	74
Exercise 37	Reported Speech — Statements	75
Exercise 38	***Would rather* • *had better***	76
Text	**Making "Small Talk"**	77
Exercise 39	Reported Speech — Questions	78
Exercise 40	Causatives *(cont'd.)*	79

Chapter 11

Dialog	**Congratulations!**	81
Culture Tip	**It Pays to Switch**	82
Exercise 41	Unreal Conditional	83
Exercise 42	***Hope* • *think* • *guess***	84
Text	**Are You a "Workaholic"?**	85
Exercise 43	It's *necessary* (*hard*, etc.) *for me* to ...	86
Exercise 44	***Such* • *so***	87

Chapter 12

Dialog	I Won't Be a Minute	89
Culture Tip	**Thanks for Not Smoking**	90
Exercise 45	Review of Tenses	91
Exercise 46	Time Expressions	92
Text	**Come Fly with Me!**	93
Exercise 47	Real vs. Unreal Conditional	94
Exercise 48	Scrambled Sentences	95

Answer Key 96
Tapescript 106

INTRODUCTION

Brush Up Your English is designed for the student who has had a good deal of prior exposure to English but who requires a systematic review and some "brushing up" before moving on. The program is designed to be used in connection with live instruction in the Berlitz classroom.

The brush-up student typically has an extensive *passive* knowledge of the language. The main objective of this program is to *activate* this knowledge and bring out a higher degree of proficiency.

Course materials include a student reader and three one-hour audio cassettes for home review. The program is divided into 12 chapters. Each chapter explores a different theme and consists of a dialog and short reading text, followed by exercises to strengthen vocabulary, structures, and practical communication skills. Each chapter also contains a "culture tip" relating to some aspect of American life and customs.

At the back of the book there is an answer key to the written exercises, along with a tapescript of the audio portion of the program. Finally, on the inside back cover there is an outline which indicates "at a glance" where particular grammar points are dealt with in the program.

Each of the three audio cassettes covers four chapters (two per side). On each tape, the dialogs of the chapter are re-enacted by a variety of professional native speakers. The student first hears the complete dialog. He then hears it again, one segment at a time, followed by a short series of comprehension questions. Finally, at the end of each tape, portions of the dialog are played through with pauses for repetition.

We have done our best to make this program both effective and interesting, to offer the brush-up student the kind of support and reinforcement so badly needed at this point in his study of English.

We are happy to add *Brush Up Your English* to the body of Berlitz instructional materials, and welcome any comments or suggestions for improvement.

CHAPTER 1

DO YOU TWO KNOW EACH OTHER?

John Morgan and his wife, Susan, are at a concert this evening. During the intermission, they go to the lobby for a soft drink.

Susan: Aren't you glad we came to the concert, John? The orchestra is terrific.

John: Well, at least I didn't fall asleep. No, really, you're absolutely right — we don't go out often enough. Hey ...!!

Lucy: Oh! I'm sorry! I didn't see you. It's orange juice ... and it's all over your jacket!

John: No problem. This jacket's been through so much already, I don't even worry about it anymore. There ... you see, it's gone now.

Lucy: Are you sure? I'm really sorry. I feel terrible.

John: It's O.K., really. No harm done. By the way, I'm John, and this is my wife, Susan.

Lucy: Nice to meet you, John, Susan. I'm Lucy.

Susan: Are you enjoying the concert, Lucy?

Lucy: Oh, yes! In fact, it's my first night out in New York. My husband, Dave, and I recently moved here from a small town in Ohio. To tell you the truth, we're still trying to get used to life in a big city.

Susan: Don't worry. You're going to love New York. Everyone does.

Lucy: I hope so. Dave's working in a big company for the first time, and he says the pressure is awful. He works late almost every night. In fact, he's calling a client right now. Can you believe it? A business call in the middle of a concert! He has a very demanding boss, and Dave is trying his best to make a good impression. It's the first time we've gone out in months.

Susan: Hmm ... that sounds familiar. I'm always trying to get John away from *his* work, too.

Lucy: Oh, here comes Dave now. Dave! Over here! Susan, John, I'd like you to meet ...

Dave: Mr. Morgan! What ... what are you doing here?

Lucy: Do you two know each other?

Dave: Sure, honey. This is my boss at Superior Products, John Morgan.

Lucy: Oh! Well ... I ... I guess it's not such a big city after all!

Friends at First Sight

One of the most difficult things to learn about another culture is its social customs — what's the polite thing to do in various situations. In the above situation, an accidental meeting takes place between John Morgan and a woman named Lucy. Morgan ends up introducing himself and his wife to Lucy, and a very friendly, even personal, conversation follows, with Lucy describing her move from Ohio and her husband's new job.

Americans often adopt a very informal manner with people, even people they have just met. They are quick to address people by their first names and often do not hesitate to discuss subjects that in some cultures might be considered too personal — family, position in a company, even politics.

SIMPLE PRESENT vs. PRESENT PROGRESSIVE

Do you **make** many phone calls?	**Are** you **making** a phone call right now?
We **don't work** on Sundays.	It's Sunday. We **aren't working** today.
Bob usually **eats** lunch at 12:00.	It's 12:00. Bob**'s eating** lunch now.

Exercise 1

Example: Would you like some coffee?
           No, thanks. ___*b*___ coffee.

a. I'm not drinking
b. I don't drink

1. Where's Jim?
   In his office. _____ on the phone.
   a. He talks
   b. He's talking

2. Could you give me a ride?
   Sure. Where _____ you _____?
   a. do ... go
   b. are ... going

3. Is the bank still open?
   Yes. It _____ open late on Fridays.
   a. stays
   b. is staying

4. May I see Mr. Morgan?
   I'm sorry. He _____ time to see you now.
   a. isn't having
   b. doesn't have

5. Excuse me, sir.
   Yes? _____ to me?
   a. Are you speaking
   b. Do you speak

6. _____ it _____ much in the summer?
   No, it's usually very nice.
   a. Does ... rain
   b. Is ... raining

7. Why _____ Pat _____ to the party?
   Because she has to work.
   a. isn't ... coming
   b. doesn't ... come

8. Are you busy?
   No, _____ anything. What do you need?
   a. I'm not doing
   b. I don't do

Exercise 2

never	seldom	sometimes
always	often	usually
ever	rarely	generally

Examples: Jim **_is always_** in the office by 9:00. *(be / always)*

He **_doesn't ever leave_** before 5:00. *(not leave / ever)*

1. Our phone _____ late at night. *(ring / rarely)*

2. Call me at 4:00. I _____ free by then. *(be / usually)*

3. _____ Harry _____ his old friends from school? *(see / ever)*

4. Prices _____ lower at that department store. *(be / generally)*

5. We _____ my parents on the weekends. *(visit / often)*

6. Jill _____ work home from the office. *(take / sometimes)*

7. The Masons _____ T.V. during the week. *(not watch / ever)*

8. _____ the 5 o'clock train _____ on time? *(be / always)*

9. The mail _____ late. *(not arrive / often)*

10. It seems like my vacations _____ long enough! *(be / never)*

11. Bob _____ the bus to work. *(take / seldom)*

12. It almost _____ in New York in April. *(snow / never)*

13. What time _____ the Bells _____ dinner? *(have / usually)*

14. The Morgans _____ to concerts. *(go / sometimes)*

15. The restaurant _____ busy at this hour. *(be / rarely)*

CHURCHILL MEETS CHURCHILL

In addition to being a great statesman, Winston Churchill was a well-known author. In the spring of 1899, he discovered that there was another writer named Winston Churchill, who lived in Boston, Massachusetts. He wrote the American Churchill a letter and sent him a copy of his latest book. He decided that in the future he would use his full name, Winston Spencer Churchill, in order to avoid confusion. But during Winston Spencer's next visit to America, the confusion of the two Churchills continued. The British Churchill's mail was sent to the American Churchill's home by mistake.

The two Churchills finally arranged to meet and have lunch. They found they had a lot in common even though they weren't related. They were both authors, and both were interested in politics. Winston Spencer was only 25 years old, but he announced with great confidence that he intended to become Prime Minister of Great Britain some day. He jokingly suggested that his new American friend go into politics as well, and try to become President of the United States.

History has forgotten the American Churchill. But the world still remembers Winston Spencer Churchill as one of the greatest political leaders of the 20th century.

INDIRECT OBJECT PRONOUNS

> Mr. Morgan is showing the office | to Dave.
>
> He's showing **him** the office.

Exercise 3

Example: Does Cindy send cards to her friends?
Yes, __she sends them cards__.

1. Have Mr. and Mrs. Bell bought a car for their son yet?
   No, _didn't buy him one_

2. Is the waiter bringing the wine for me and my wife?
   Yes, _he brings us wine_

3. Did you leave a message for Mrs. Williams?
   Yes, _I left it her_

4. Have I shown the memo to you?
   Yes, _I shown it you_

5. Is the hostess serving coffee to the Jeffersons?
   No, _she isn't coffee to them_

6. Would the salesman like to sell a car to John?
   Yes, _he would like to sell him one_

7. Did Bob give his phone number to you?
   No, _he didn't gave it to you_

8. Will Laura mail her pictures to you and Jim?
   Yes, _she will mail them her pict._

9. Did Mr. Jensen offer the job to Frank?
   Yes, _he did offer to him_

10. Has Janet written a letter to her sister lately?
    No, _she hasn't written her a letter_

STILL • ANYMORE

> Do you still live in the same apartment?
> – Yes, I **still** live there.
> – No, I don't live there **anymore**.

Exercise 4

Examples: Was it still raining when you came in? *(Yes)*
Yes, it was still raining when I came in.

Does Jim still work for a large company? *(No)*
No, he doesn't work for a large company anymore.

1. Are we still supposed to have a meeting next Friday? *(Yes)*
2. Is Mr. Jenkins still out of town on business? *(Yes)*
3. Do you still play tennis? *(No)*
4. Was Mr. Lee still busy with a client when you called? *(Yes)*
5. Does Tom still smoke? *(No)*
6. Do the accountants still have to work Saturdays? *(No)*
7. When you met her, was Jill still working at the bank? *(No)*
8. Are you still waiting to see Mrs. Drake? *(Yes)*
9. Were the packages still by the door when you left? *(Yes)*
10. Does the Number 5 bus still stop at the corner of 17th and Elm? *(No)*
11. Was Paula still thinking about changing jobs when you saw her? *(Yes)*
12. Do you and Frank Collins still keep in touch? *(No)*

CHAPTER 2

WHEN CAN WE GET TOGETHER?

Jim Reynolds works in the Marketing Department at Superior Products. He wants to get in touch with John Morgan to talk over some ideas he has for a new advertising campaign. He called Morgan's office first thing in the morning, hoping to catch him before he got tied up.

Janet: Mr. Morgan's office. May I help you?

Jim: Janet, this is Jim Reynolds. I'd like to talk to John if he's free.

Janet: Oh, hello, Mr. Reynolds. I'm sorry, he was in earlier, but he had to leave for a meeting. He should be back around 11 o'clock.

Jim: Just my luck! I really wanted to get hold of him to set up a meeting for today or tomorrow. When he gets back, could you ask him to return my call?

Janet: Sure. I'll give him the message as soon as he gets in.

When Mr. Morgan returned, Janet gave him the message and he returned Jim's call right away.

Secretary: Good morning, Jim Reynold's office.

John: This is John Morgan returning his call. Is he in?

Secretary: Yes, he is, Mr. Morgan. He's expecting your call. He's on the other line right now. Would you like to hold or can he call you back?

John: I'll hold.

(a moment later)

Jim: Hi, John. Sorry to keep you waiting. Listen, I'd like to get together and discuss some ideas for the new ad campaign. Could we possibly meet tomorrow morning?

John: Sorry, Jim, I've got a 9 o'clock appointment and I may be tied up all morning. How about lunch? We can grab a quick sandwich at that little place around the corner. About 12:30?

Jim: Great. See you then.

Let's Grab a Bite

culture tip

Business is often conducted on an informal basis, particularly when people know each other well. Mr. Morgan and Mr. Reynolds are close business associates. They're on a first-name basis, and Reynolds is able to set up an informal lunch appointment on very short notice. It is not at all unusual for Americans to conduct business over a light lunch — sometimes right in the office! In this instance, however, Morgan and Reynolds decide to "grab a quick sandwich" at a little place around the corner.

CAN • SHOULD • MAY • MUST

> **May** I see your plane tickets, please?
> You **should** go to the boarding area in 10 minutes.
> This bag is too big. You **can't** carry it on board.
> You **must** show your boarding passes to the attendant.

Exercise 5

Jack: Good morning. __May__ (Must / May) I speak to Mr. Harris, please?

Secretary: I'm sorry. He _____ (can't / mustn't) come to the phone right now. _____ (May / Should) I take a message?

Jack: I _____ (must / may) get hold of him today. It's very important.

Secretary: _____ (Can / Must) you hold on? I think I hear him coming.

Jack: Sure. Thank you.

Ed: Hi, Jack! What's up?

Jack: Listen. There's a big problem with the Larsen account. I just _____ (shouldn't / can't) figure it out! What do you think I _____ (should / may) do?

Ed: The Larsen account? Well, one thing you _____ (can't / shouldn't) do is worry. I was about to call you. The reason you _____ (mustn't / can't) figure it out is that the figures they gave us aren't accurate.

Jack: What?! No wonder I _____ (can't / mustn't) get it to work out. Thanks for telling me!

EXPRESSING PROBABILITY

> The weather is bad, so Tim's flight **might** not get in on time.
> It's almost 6:00. **Shouldn't** Julie be home by now?
> Be careful! You **could** hurt yourself!
> We **may** go to the beach next weekend if it's nice.
> Frank walks to work. He **must** live near his office.

Exercise 6

Example: (might / must)
Take an umbrella. It ___*might*___ rain today.

1. (should / must)
   You _____ be tired after such a long drive.

2. (may not / shouldn't)
   It's 4:45. We _____ make it to the bank before it closes.

3. (could / should)
   John isn't here yet. I guess he _____ be tied up in traffic.

4. (may not / must not)
   You'd better take some cash. The restaurant _____ take credit cards.

5. (must / could)
   Laura talks about her job a lot. She _____ enjoy her work.

6. (could / may)
   Where _____ Bob be? He's already an hour late!

7. (shouldn't / may not)
   Here's $10. The supplies _____ cost more than that.

8. (should / might)
   The Wilsons _____ go to England next summer, but they aren't sure.

9. (must not / might not)
   If we don't hurry, we _____ get to the airport in time.

10. (couldn't / must not)
    I called Ted, but there was no answer. He _____ be home.

PSYCHO-SELL: ARE YOU IMMUNE?

One of the most effective ways companies get us to buy their products is by establishing a link between what they're selling and what we need. This is the key to effective advertising.

One kind of advertising is "psycho-sell," and it's aimed at our most personal feelings. For example, some of the most successful psycho-sell ads have been used to sell "personal care" products. Consumers who never worried about bad breath before are suddenly convinced they need mouthwash. And for those who want to stay young forever, there are dozens of creams and lotions that promise to stop, or even reverse, the aging process.

Some advertising campaigns are directed at our insecurities. They suggest that fast food, soft drinks, and a good laundry detergent are the keys to a happy family life. They also tell us that if we want to be a success in life, we have to have designer clothes, the "right" car, and the latest electronic gadget. Although we may think we're immune to psycho-sell, research shows that it is extremely effective. After all, who wants to stay unhappy if happiness is available for $1.29 at the local pharmacy?

Exercise 7

A. Fill in **some**, **any**, **a lot**, or **no**.

Example: Were there __*any*__ calls while I was out?

1. We aren't expecting _____ news about the contract until Friday.
2. Jim is never without a cigarette. He sure smokes _____ !
3. There isn't _____ coffee left. Should I make _____ ?
4. Carl plans to catch up on _____ paperwork this afternoon.
5. I thought I'd have _____ messages, but there weren't _____ .
6. Give me a call if you have _____ questions about the conference.
7. Sue had to use her credit card because she had _____ money left.
8. We've been having _____ of problems with the copy machine.

B. Fill in **much**, **many**, **a few**, or **a little**.

Example: I don't have __*much*__ money. I'd better cash a check.

1. Phil says he's making _____ progress in Spanish, but not _____ .
2. How _____ time do we have before the bus leaves?
3. Mrs. Drake would like to see you when you have _____ minutes.
4. We haven't gotten _____ responses to our advertisement.
5. How _____ people does the department want to hire?
6. There are _____ cars Tom would like to own, but only _____ he can afford.
7. The aspirin helped _____ , but I still have a headache.
8. Julie knows a lot of French, but she doesn't know _____ German.

Exercise 8

A. *Example:* Does Ed want to buy a new car? Can he afford to?
He wants to buy a new car, but he can't afford to.

1. Do the Blakes want to move to London? Can they do it this year?

2. Can Jane swim? Does she like to swim in the ocean?

3. Should we make reservations? Do we have to make them a month in advance?

4. Must you leave soon? Do you have to leave right now?

5. Does Frank like to drive fast? Should he?

6. Should Paula work on the report? Does she want to do it now?

7. Should you go to the meeting? Do you have to?

8. Does Sam like to play football? Can he play this Sunday?

B. *Examples:* What __do__ you like to do on weekends?
What movie __would__ you like to see tonight?

1. _____ you like Mr. Morgan to return your call?

2. Why _____ Bill like to get to work so early on Mondays?

3. Where _____ the Randalls like to spend their summers?

4. How soon _____ Jim like to get started on the ad campaign?

5. What kind of car _____ Mary like to buy?

6. _____ Gary and his wife like to watch T.V. in the evenings?

7. What day _____ you like to leave for Boston?

8. _____ Janet like to do her shopping on Saturdays?

CHAPTER 3

BACK ALREADY?

Janet is in the company cafeteria. She's just paid for her food and is looking for a place to sit when she notices her friend Bob Elliott sitting alone at a table in the corner.

Janet: Hey, Bob! I thought you were on vacation.

Bob: I was, but I came back last night. I was only away for three days. They had an emergency in the office, and my boss called and asked if I could cut my vacation short. It's too bad I left my number with his secretary!

Janet: Where did you go?

Bob: To Washington. I have friends there, and they invited me to come down and spend some time with them.

Janet: Washington? Really? I went to college there. What did you see? Did you visit the White House?

Bob: We sure did. Then we drove around and visited all the famous tourist sights. I think it's a great city!

Janet: I do, too. Did you get to see the Picasso exhibit at the National Gallery? There was a big article about it in the *New York Times* last Sunday.

Bob: We tried, but it was too crowded. The line stretched halfway around the block. We visited the Air and Space Museum instead. What a place! We were there almost four hours, and we didn't even see half of it. Then, that night, my friends fixed me up with a date and we went out to a disco. We didn't get back till three in the morning.

Janet: It sounds like you had quite a time!

Bob: I did. But I learned one lesson ... when you take your vacation, don't tell your boss where you're going!

How Much Vacation?

culture tip

The amount of vacation time for employees varies greatly from country to country. In most European countries, even a new employee can expect to have at least a month's vacation after working one year. The United States is much more conservative: after a year on the job, most employees can expect no more than two weeks' paid vacation, sometimes less. It may be 20 years before an employee has "earned" a month's vacation — although, in addition to vacation time, most companies allow 2 – 3 "personal days" to be taken at the discretion of the employee.

Exercise 9

JOHN MORGAN'S DAY

Every day, John **gets up** at 6:30. He **takes** a shower, **shaves**, and **gets dressed**; then he **has** breakfast. He **doesn't eat** much — just toast, juice, and coffee. He **leaves** the house about 7:45 and **catches** the 8 o'clock train. His secretary, Janet, **comes** in earlier than he **does**; so when he **gets** there, she**'s** already at her desk. She **opens** the mail and **brings** it to him, and **gives** him his messages. He**'s** very busy — he **makes** a lot of phone calls and **sees** several clients. After lunch, he **writes** a few memos and **gives** them to Janet to type. He **meets** with his marketing director and then **reads** the latest sales reports. At 5:00, he **says** good night to Janet and **goes** home. On the way home, he **stops** to buy the evening paper. He and his wife **don't have** dinner until 7:00, so he **has** time to sit down and watch the news. After a long day at the office, he **feels** like relaxing.

Rewrite the text in the past tense.

Yesterday, John **got up** at 6:30. He took a shower, shaved, and got dressed then he had breakfast. He didn't eat much — just toast, juice, and coffee. He left the house about 7:45 and caught the 8 o'clock train. His secretary, Janet, came in earlier than he did, so when he got there, she was already at her desk. She opened the mail and brought it to him, and gave him his messages. He was very busy he made a lot of phone calls and saw several clients. After lunch he wrote a few memos and gave them to Janet to type. He met with his marketing director and then read the latest sales reports. At 5:00 he said good night to Janet and went home. On the way home, he stopped to buy the evening paper. He and his wife didn't have dinner until 7:00, so he had time to sit down and watch the news. After a long day at the office he felt like relaxing.

Exercise 10

Examples: Jim's apartment has three bedrooms. What about yours?
Mine does, too.

Mary didn't enjoy the movie. What about you?
I didn't, either.

1. We should go to the meeting tomorrow. What about Mr. Turner?
   He should, too
2. I don't have to work on Saturday. What about Laura?
   She doesn't either
3. Bill wasn't in New York last week. What about you and your wife?
   We wasn't either
4. Paris has many interesting sights. What about Rome?
   Rome does, too
5. My company opened an office in Toronto. What about Bert's?
   Bert's did, too
6. Frank wants to play golf this weekend. What about his friends?
   His friend do, too
7. We shouldn't be gone very long. What about Cindy?
   Cindy shouldn't either
8. The trains are running behind schedule. What about the buses?
   The buses are, too
9. Ted can help us move the furniture. What about Joe?
   Joe can't either, too
10. Our car won't start in cold weather. What about Jim's?
    Jim's won't, too
11. I didn't get any mail yesterday. What about you?
    I didn't either
12. You went to work yesterday. What about Janet?
    Janet did, too
13. The Gordons are coming to the party. What about the Millers?
    Millers are, too
14. I don't enjoy going to movies. What about my wife?
    My wife doesn't either
15. Jim wasn't at work yesterday. What about Sam and Gina?
    They weren't either

JAMES MACIE'S WILL

James Macie was born in France in 1765, the illegitimate son of an English duke, Sir Hugh Percy Smithson. Macie later became a naturalized British subject; but, because of his questionable past, he was never completely accepted into British society. Using his mother's family name, Macie did eventually become a respected chemist and, in the end, inherited the family's substantial fortune.

But James Macie still had bitter feelings toward the country that had turned its back on him. When he made out his will in 1826, he got his revenge by leaving his entire fortune to the government of the United States, a country he had never even visited. And to add insult to injury, he adopted his father's name, Smithson, in his will. He ordered that his entire estate of $500,000 be used to create a new national museum, to be named after him, in Washington, D.C.

In 1846, the Smithsonian Institution was established according to James Macie Smithson's wishes. Its twelve museums, including the National Gallery of Art and the Natural History Museum, contain huge cultural, historical, and scientific collections. It is, in fact, the world's largest museum complex, and its Air and Space Museum alone attracts 10 million visitors a year.

POSSESSIVE ADJECTIVES AND PRONOUNS

	my			mine.
	your			yours.
	his			his.
This is	her	car.	It's	hers.
	our			ours.
	their			theirs.

Exercise 11

Example: I've finished __my__ report. Has Maria finished __hers__?

1. Jim bought __his__ computer in April, and I bought __mine__ in May.
2. __Our__ electric bill surprised us last month. Did you find __yours__ was high, too?
3. What's Ellen going to give __her__ husband for __his__ birthday?
4. That's Julie's hat, and the raincoat is __hers__, too.
5. The Blakes are renting a car while __theirs__ is being repaired.
6. Jack has __his__ exercise class on Tuesday nights, but Laura and I have __ours__ on Thursdays.
7. Even though __their__ train was late, Bob and Sam got to work on time.
8. Did the Coopers take __their__ vacation the same week Paul took __his__?
9. May I use __your__ pen, Bill? I forgot __mine__.
10. Do Frank and __his__ wife still live around the corner from you?
11. Tom and I got the wrong coats. He picked up __mine__ coat, and I got __his__.
12. __Your__ car is blocking __mine__. Would you mind moving it?

Exercise 12

Fill in the simple present or past tense of the verb in parentheses.

Examples: Jerry **_goes_** to the movies once a week. *(go)*

What movie **_did_** he **_see_** last week? *(see)*

1. The mail usually _arrives_ at 12:30, but it's late today. *(arrive)*
2. _Does_ Paula still _work_ at the bank? *(work)*
3. After looking all over, I _found_ my keys in my coat pocket. *(find)*
4. Tim _doesn't get_ a chance to see his family very often. *(not get)*
5. _Were_ you _able to_ get hold of Mr. Parker yesterday? *(be able to)*
6. I _spoke_ to John a couple of days ago, and I _gave_ him your message. *(speak / give)*
7. Who _taught_ Susan how to drive? *(teach)*
8. When I _broke_ my leg, I _couldn't walk_ for two months. *(break / can't walk)*
9. How long ago _did_ Mary _get back_ from her vacation? *(get back)*
10. _Did it_ it usually _take_ a week to get film developed? *(take)*
11. I _don't drink_ coffee in the evening because it _keeps_ me up at night. *(not drink / keep)*
12. When _did_ Superior Products first _opened_ their London office? *(open)*
13. Bob's team _lost_ the basketball game by 2 points. *(lose)*
14. What _did_ the Millers _do_ last weekend? *(do)*
15. How often _did / does_ the marketing director _met_ with his staff? *(meet)*

CHAPTER

I'D LIKE TO SPEAK TO THE MANAGER

Janet is in Los Angeles visiting her sister. She has just arrived at the airport and is standing at the car rental counter.

Janet: Hello, I'm Janet Brown. I have a reservation for a compact car.

Agent: Fine. Let's see ... when did you make the reservation?

Janet: It was last Wednesday, I think.

Agent: O.K., let me check. Hmm, are you sure you made the reservation with this agency? The computer isn't showing anything in your name.

Janet: Yes, I'm positive. I called your toll-free number.

Agent: We've had some trouble with the computer lately ... but it doesn't matter. We still have quite a few cars available.

Janet: They promised a compact car would be waiting for me when I got here.

Agent: A compact? I'm sorry, but all our compacts are out. The only thing we have left is a full-size sedan. It's only nineteen dollars a day more than the compact.

Janet: But, that's ridiculous! I don't need a full-size car, and I'm certainly not going to pay more for one. I reserved a compact, and that's what I want!

Agent: But I've already explained, we don't have any compacts available. There's really nothing I can do. You know, our full-size cars are really very nice. They're more comfortable and much more luxurious. And if you think about it, bigger cars are safer.

Janet: Look, why don't you just let me speak to the manager?

Agent: All right, I'll see if he's free.

(a few minutes later)

Agent: I'm sorry, Mr. Stephens is tied up right now. But because of the mix-up, he's agreed to let you have a full-size car for the same price as a compact.

Janet: Well ... I appreciate that. Hmm ... it looks like I'll be driving around in style. Oh, by the way, you don't have a red car by any chance, do you? That's my favorite color ...

Stick to Your Guns

Culture tip

Arguing with clerks and other customer service people has become a part of life in every country. In the dialog, Janet was the victim of a computer foul-up. The problem was not really the fault of the employee.

But Janet was firm and stood up for her rights, even when the clerk said there was nothing he could do. Finally, she asked to see the manager.

THE PRESENT PERFECT

Finished Time	Unfinished Time
I **spoke** to Sue last week.	I'**ve spoken** to her this week.
Did you **see** Ed yesterday?	**Have** you **seen** him today?
I **didn't go** to Rome last year.	I'**ve** never **been** to Rome.
Why **didn't** Bill **call** this morning?	Why **hasn't** he **called** yet?

Exercise 13

Fill in the correct form of the present perfect.

Example: Carl and Peter **have been** friends for years. *(be)*

1. We _____ plans for the holidays yet. *(not make)*

2. _____ anyone _____ Ken since he got back from France? *(hear from)*

3. How long _____ Mr. Wilson _____ high school? *(teach)*

4. Mrs. Phillips _____ just _____ her secretary some letters to type. *(give)*

5. The office _____ never _____ as busy as it was last Friday! *(be)*

6. The Lees _____ several houses, but they _____ one yet. *(look at / not buy)*

7. _____ you ever _____ at a restaurant called *La Cocina*? *(eat)*

8. So far, we _____ good luck with our car. *(have)*

9. Kenny _____ here yet. I wonder what's keeping him. *(not get)*

10. Why _____ you and John _____ to visit lately? *(not stop by)*

11. Jim's company _____ business with us for years. *(do)*

12. _____ anyone _____ Frank about the meeting? *(not tell)*

Exercise 14

Fill in **yet**, **already**, **for**, or **since**.

Example: Bob hasn't taken a vacation ___*for*___ two years.

1. Jack sent the package a week ago, but it hasn't arrived _____.

2. The weather has been beautiful _____ the beginning of April.

3. Have you talked to Lois _____ she started working?

4. I'm sorry. Mr. Morgan has _____ left for the day.

5. Have Mr. and Mrs. Spencer lived in London _____ a long time?

6. We've _____ seen that movie, and we don't want to see it again.

7. The mail hasn't come _____, but I'll let you know when it does.

8. Jerry and I have known each other _____ we were in college.

9. Jill hasn't gotten a letter from her sister _____ several weeks.

10. I haven't even had time to read the newspaper _____.

11. The waiter has _____ served us coffee, but he hasn't brought our desserts _____.

12. How long has it been _____ you saw your brother?

13. The new bakery has been open _____ three weeks.

14, Sue bought a book yesterday, and she's finished it _____!

15. Has Mary's French improved _____ she started taking lessons?

CALIFORNIA — FANTASYLAND

In the 16th century, Spanish novelist Garcí Ordoñez de Montalvo described an imaginary island full of gold and precious jewels and called it *California*. In 1533, an early Spanish explorer of the western coast of the United States was so impressed by the area's beauty that he named it after Ordoñez de Montalvo's make-believe island.

And so, from the beginning, California was built on illusion. And when large deposits of gold were discovered there in 1849, tens of thousands of eager prospectors streamed into the area. (To this day, California is still called the "Golden State.")

More recently, America's motion picture industry, centered in Hollywood, has delighted audiences with the dreamworld it has created. California is also home to Disneyland, where fantasy comes true for millions of children and adults every year.

It's not surprising that California has often been in the forefront of social change. This land of dreamers has led the way in everything from the latest fashions to the most advanced computer technology. Skate-boarding, blue jeans, and pop psychology all got their start there. The "Golden State" of California has truly lived up to its name, far surpassing the imaginary island that Ordoñez de Montalvo described over three centuries ago.

Exercise 15

Fill in the simple present, simple past, or present perfect.

Examples: How long **does** it usually **take** you to drive to work? *(take)*
Bruce **hasn't been** to Europe since 1984. *(not be)*
Sarah **visited** her uncle when she was in New York. *(visit)*

1. _Has_ Patty _made_ plans for the weekend yet? *(make)*

2. I _was_ late to work yesterday because my alarm _didn't ring_. *(be / not ring)*

3. Why _did_ Scott _quit_ his job last week? *(quit)*

4. The Randalls _don't live_ in London anymore. *(not live)*

5. How many games _have_ the soccer team _won_ so far? *(win)*

6. Mr. Tucker always _reads_ the paper every morning at breakfast. *(read)*

7. I _meant_ to call you last Sunday, but I completely _forgot_ about it. *(mean / forget)*

8. We _haven't seen_ Jim and Sue since they _got_ married. *(not see / get)*

9. The post office _doesn't deliver_ mail on holidays. *(not deliver)*

10. _Did_ you _learn_ to speak German when you _lived_ in Bonn? *(learn / live)*

11. I _have_ never _understood_ how electricity _works_. *(understand / work)*

12. How often _does_ Janet _see_ her family? *(see)*

13. It _hasn't rained_ for several weeks now. *(not rain)*

14. _Do_ you and Nancy still _play_ a lot of tennis? *(play)*

15. Mr. Kelly _retired_ a month ago, and the company _hasn't replaced_ him yet. *(retire / not replace)*

COMPARATIVES • SUPERLATIVES

> It's **hotter** today **than** it was yesterday.
> What's **the quickest** way to get to Bob's house?
> The Savoy is **the best** hotel in the city.
> Do you think Vienna is **as beautiful as** Paris?
> Computers are getting **more sophisticated** every year.

Exercise 16

Examples: Jim is one of **the nicest** people I've ever met. *(nice)*

Sit here. The sofa is **more comfortable than** that chair. *(comfortable)*

1. February is often _the coldest_ month of the year. *(cold)*
2. Won't we get there a lot _faster_ if we go by taxi? *(fast)*
3. A gold ring is _more valuable_ a silver one. *(valuable)*
4. Which city is _farther_ from here, Boston or Toronto? *(far)*
5. Jack has lost weight. He doesn't look _as heavy_ he used to. *(heavy)*
6. That was _the most ex_ football game I've ever seen! *(exciting)*
7. I took the position because it was _more than_ my old job. *(challenging)*
8. Today is miserable! I hope the weather is _better_ tomorrow. *(good)*
9. At one time, the Butlers were _the wealthiest_ family in the city. *(wealthy)*
10. John doesn't play tennis nearly _as well as_ his brother. *(well)*
11. Of the author's three books, his second one was _the best_. *(good)*
12. Speaking Japanese isn't _more of_ writing it. *(difficult)*

CHAPTER 5

WHAT'S GOING ON OUT THERE?

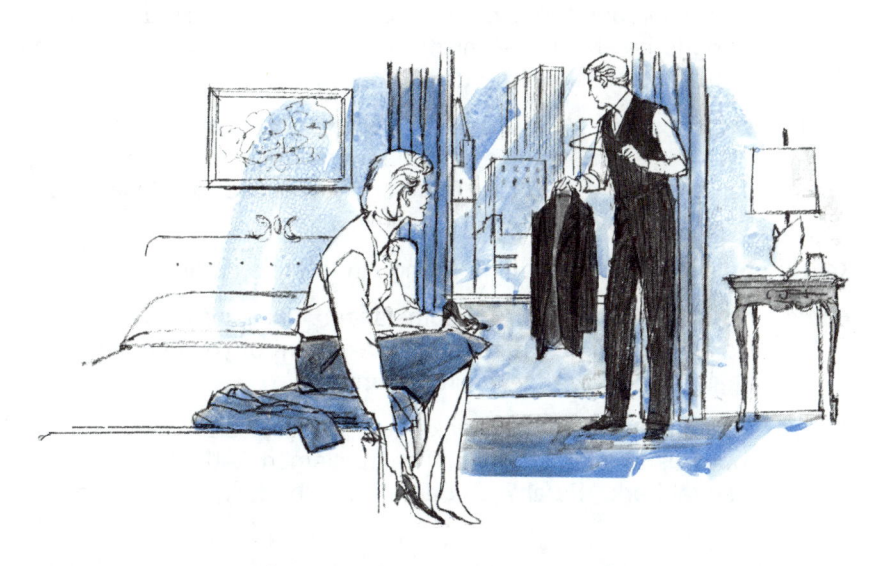

Kevin Williams, manager of Superior Products' London office, is in New York on business for a few days. Right now, he and his wife, Sarah, are in their hotel room.

Kevin: This is a much better hotel than the one we stayed at last time, don't you think, Sarah?

Sarah: Oh, yes, it's very nice. Goodness, what a trip! We've been up since five this morning. And I didn't get a wink of sleep on the plane. I think I'll take a short nap.

Kevin: That sounds like a good idea. A little sleep and we'll be as good as new. Can you believe it's only 10:30 in the morning here? I certainly don't feel like doing much today. I think the jetlag is getting to me already.

Sarah: Kevin, do you hear that dreadful pounding noise? What *ever* are they doing out there?

Kevin: Hmm ... it sounds as if they're tearing up the street.

Sarah: Just what we needed! We'll never get any sleep if that keeps up. Do you think we should see if they can give us a different room?

Kevin: Good idea. I'll call the front desk.

Clerk: Front desk. May I help you?

Kevin: This is Kevin Williams in Room 217. There's a lot of pounding going on outside our window. My wife and I are quite tired, and we're not going to be able to get much rest with all that commotion going on. Could you possibly give us another room?

Clerk: Oh, I'm sorry, Mr. Williams. They're doing some construction across the street. I'm sure we can arrange something. Let's see ... yes, I can give you a very nice room on the 7th floor overlooking Central Park. It's very quiet, and the view is lovely.

Kevin: Splendid. There'll be no change in the rate, I hope.

Clerk: No, sir. Not under the circumstances. I'll send the bellman right up. He'll show you to the room and take care of your luggage. And, once again, I apologize for the inconvenience.

Kevin: That's quite all right. Thank you. ... Well, Sarah, they're going to move us to another room. The gentleman said it has a lovely view of Central Park. Sarah? ... Sarah? ... Oh, dear, she's fallen asleep!

Combining Business with Pleasure

culture tip

In the world of business, the role of a person's wife or husband varies greatly from country to country. Although most business people travel alone, it is not unusual for the spouse to go along. In this way, they can combine business with pleasure, perhaps staying over a weekend to allow time for a little shopping or sightseeing.

Spouses are often included in social events sponsored by the company. And it is not unusual to invite a business associate, or even a client, home for dinner.

FUTURE TIME

> We're **flying** to Philadelphia tomorrow.
> Our plane **leaves** at 9 in the morning.
> The hotel limousine **will pick** us **up** at the airport.
> We're **going to take** a tour of the city.
> There **won't be** time to see everything we'd like.

Exercise 17

Example: I'll call you tomorrow morning. *(When?)*
When will you call me?

1. The bank is going to close in a few minutes. *(How soon?)*

2. Janice has to get up at 5:30 tomorrow morning. *(What time?)*

3. We're going to stay at the Regency Hotel. *(Where?)*

4. Mr. Reeves will be out of town for 2 weeks. *(How long?)*

5. Tom is taking Gloria out to dinner Friday night. *(When?)*

6. It'll cost at least $100 to get the T.V. repaired. *(How much?)*

7. My French class begins next week. *(When?)*

8. The Bakers are taking the 6:15 train. *(Which?)*

9. Ellen is going to meet us at the theater. *(Where?)*

10. I won't have time to finish the report because I have a meeting. *(Why?)*

11. Gary's plane gets in at 7 this evening. *(What time?)*

12. Bill is going to borrow a friend's typewriter. *(Whose?)*

COMBINING SENTENCES

> I'll give you a call. **I'll be** in New York.
>
> I'll give you a call *when I'm* in New York.

If Janet **has to** work late, she won't go to the movies.
Will you shop around *before* you **buy** a car?
Ted will stop by the office *after* he **goes** to the bank.

Exercise 18

Example: (not be able to / rain)
Paul **won't be able to** play tennis tomorrow if it **rains**.

1. (leave / meet)
   Before Mrs. Bell _____ this afternoon, she _____ with Mr. Chase.

2. (wear / go out)
   What _____ Lois _____ when she _____ tonight?

3. (miss / not get on)
   Mary _____ her connection if she _____ this flight.

4. (get / order)
   As soon as Jim _____ here, we _____ dinner.

5. (finish / look for)
   After Carol _____ school, she _____ a job in advertising.

6. (not come / come)
   If the repairman _____ today, he _____ tomorrow.

7. (change / charge)
   If we _____ rooms, _____ they _____ us extra?

8. (open / not have)
   When the new office _____, we _____ phones for a few days.

9. (call / arrives)
   Phillip _____ his brother as soon as he _____ in London.

10. (wait / not be)
    If we _____ for the next train, maybe it _____ so crowded.

TIMING IS EVERYTHING!

Do you ever wish your biological clock were as easy to reset as your watch? Well, I do — every time I come down with a bad case of jet lag after getting off a long international flight. My body clock gets "scrambled," and I don't know when I'm supposed to be hungry or tired. Inevitably, if I arrive at my destination ready for a good night's sleep, my itinerary says I'm due at an all-day meeting. And that's not all — when everyone else is ready for bed, *my* body clock shouts "Let's have a party!"

Eating is another activity that causes rescheduling problems. Either I'm too tired to stay awake through a meal, or my stomach growls so loudly in the middle of the night that it wakes me up! But when I do finally start getting hungry at normal mealtimes, I know I'm on the road to recovery at last.

And then, after four or five days, there's that special morning when my alarm clock says it's time to get up, and my biological clock agrees. Everything starts to run smoothly — I'm back on schedule again. But wouldn't you know it? That's the very day I leave for home ... and start the terrible process all over again!

Exercise 19

A. Fill in **too** or **enough** plus the adjective.

   Example: If you're __too warm__ , I can open the window. *(warm)*

   1. This shirt is _____ . Do you have it in a larger size? *(small)*

   2. The conference room is the only room _____ for a meeting. *(large)*

   3. Will Jimmy be _____ to start school next year? *(old)*

   4. Sue and Jeff had to stop playing tennis because it got _____ . *(dark)*

   5. That's a dangerous road. It's barely _____ for two cars. *(wide)*

   6. We couldn't get on the bus because it was _____ . *(crowded)*

B. Fill in **too much, too many,** or **enough**.

   Example: This tea tastes awful! It has __too much__ sugar in it.

   1. I don't want to leave now. There's _____ traffic at this time of day.

   2. Will a half hour be _____ time for you to get ready?

   3. Bill can't get to sleep because he drank _____ coffee.

   4. Sara never shops on Saturdays because there are _____ people in the stores.

   5. Is there _____ pie for everyone to have a piece?

   6. Do you know the saying "_____ cooks spoil the soup"?

GERUNDS AFTER PREPOSITIONS

> First we checked into the hotel. Then we had lunch.
> → We checked into the hotel before **having** lunch.
>
> Bill got to the airport on time. He was worried about it.
> → He was worried about **getting** there on time.
>
> I'll see Jim when I'm in New York. I plan on it.
> → I plan on **seeing** Jim when I'm in New York.

Exercise 20

Examples: Jim was fired. He stole money from the company. *(for)*
Jim was fired for stealing money from the company.

I got a refund. I insisted on it. *(on)*
I insisted on getting a refund.

1. We had dinner. Then we went to the movies. *(before)*

2. Janet got a raise. She worked very hard. *(by)*

3. You can't learn a second language. You have to study. *(without)*

4. I'll see you next week. I'm looking forward to it. *(to)*

5. Billy got sick. He ate too much candy. *(from)*

6. Tom left early. He apologized for it. *(for)*

7. Janet starts her new job next week. She's all excited about it. *(about)*

8. Kevin is a top student in his class. He's proud of it. *(of)*

9. The Whites might buy a bigger house. They've talked about it. *(about)*

10. We'll order dinner. Then we'll have a glass of wine. *(after)*

CHAPTER 6

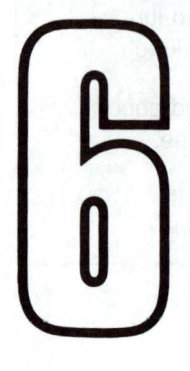

I'LL TAKE IT!

Mr. Morgan was reading the newspaper one day and saw that *Macy's* was having a big sale on men's clothes. He went to the store at lunch time, and a salesman came up to him.

Salesman: May I help you with something?

Mr. Morgan: Yes. I see you're having a sale on sports jackets.

Salesman: That's right. All our jackets are on sale for the next three days. Were you looking for anything in particular?

Mr. Morgan: Well, a few minutes ago you were showing a gentleman a dark blue winter jacket. I was thinking of something along those lines.

Salesman: That's a very popular jacket. We've been selling quite a few of them lately. What size do you wear?

Mr. Morgan: I take a 40 regular.

Salesman: All the 40's are on this rack over here. This is the one the gentleman was trying on. It's 100% English wool.

Mr. Morgan: I like the style. It's not a bad color, either. I also like this gray one here. I'd like to try both on, if I can.

Salesman: Certainly. The mirror is over there in the corner, by the window.

(Mr. Morgan tries on the blue jacket.)

Salesman: Well, how does it feel?

Mr. Morgan: It feels a little small. Maybe I should try it in a larger size.

Salesman: I'm sorry. We don't have that color in size 42. But we do have the gray one in that size. Would you like to try it on?

Mr. Morgan: All right. Ah ... this one fits much better. Yes, it's perfect. I think I'll take it!

Salesman: Will that be cash or charge?

Mr. Morgan: Charge, please.

Salesman: Fine. Oh, by the way, if you'd like to look at some shirts to go with that, there's a very good sale going on in the shirt department.

Mr. Morgan: Thanks. I'll have a look.

Cash or Charge?

"Cash or charge?" You'll hear this question almost every time you buy something in the United States. But there are actually three choices: cash, charge, or personal check. Credit cards are most frequently used in hotels, restaurants, car rental agencies, department stores, gas stations, and the like. Purchases at small local stores can often be paid for by personal check, but only when the check is from a local bank and when the person writing the check has the "proper" identification (usually a driver's license and/or a major credit card). Cash is generally used for smaller, miscellaneous purchases.

Credit cards are in wide use in the United States and are available to young people almost as soon as they begin working. Many people have personal checking accounts even before they finish school.

THE PAST PROGRESSIVE

> At 8:00 last night, the Morgans **were watching** T.V.
> What did John do while Susan **was shopping**?
> Carl **was having** dinner when his friends stopped by.

Exercise 21

Example: Mary __*was playing*__ the piano when I __***arrived***__ . (play / arrive)

1. Where _____ Jack _____ when you _____ him? *(go / see)*
2. When I _____ to Joyce, she _____ moving to Miami.
   (talk / think about)
3. _____ you _____ a part-time job while you _____ the university? *(have / attend)*
4. The fire alarm _____ while we _____ our English test.
   (go off / take)
5. _____ it _____ when you _____ this morning?
   (snow / get up)
6. I _____ an old friend while I _____ down the street.
   (run into / walk)
7. Bob _____ where he was going when he _____ the accident.
   (not watch / have)
8. We _____ leave the party because we _____ such a good time.
   (not want to / have)
9. The phone _____ three times while Ed _____ a nap. *(ring / take)*
10. Janet _____ her eyes closed while the plane _____ .
    (keep / land)
11. I _____ Jim's car because my brother _____ mine.
    (borrow / use)
12. _____ someone _____ for Mrs. Bell when her train _____ ?
    (wait / arrive)

PRESENT PERFECT PROGRESSIVE

> John **is working** on a report.
> **I'm waiting** for Ed.
> **Are** you **studying** French?
> ⇨
> He**'s been working** on it for hours.
> **I've been waiting** for him since 9.
> How long **have** you **been studying** it?

Exercise 22

Example: (is typing / has been typing)
Janet **_has been typing_** all morning.

1. (is ... working / has ... been working)
   How long _____ Kevin _____ for Superior Products?

2. (I'm listening / I've been listening)
   Please be quiet! _____ to the news.

3. (aren't playing / haven't been playing)
   Bob and Linda _____ much tennis anymore.

4. (isn't feeling / hasn't been feeling)
   Paul's father _____ well for the past few months.

5. (are ... doing / have ... been doing)
   What _____ you _____ since the last time I saw you?

6. (is ... sitting / has ... been sitting)
   Excuse me, _____ someone _____ here?

7. (I'm trying / I've been trying)
   _____ to reach Mr. Taylor since noon, but no one answers.

8. (aren't ... getting / haven't ... been getting)
   Why _____ the employees _____ a raise this year?

9. (We're meaning to / We've been meaning to)
   _____ stop by for a visit, but we've been too busy.

10. (are ... living / have ... been living)
    How long _____ the Morgans _____ in New York?

SEE YOU AT THE MALL!

Teenage girls stroll along, talking and giggling and trying to get the attention of a group of boys. An elderly woman sits resting on a bench, watching people pass by. Young mothers push baby carriages, men stand waiting impatiently for their wives, and everyone is loaded down with as many packages as they can carry. The sounds of people talking, music playing, and cash registers ringing are everywhere. Do you know where we are? Well, we're at "the mall," and it could be anywhere in the world.

Today's shopping malls are more than just marketplaces. They're gathering places for people of all ages and centers of community life. Students gather at the small cafés of the *Forum Les Halles* in Paris. The huge West Edmonton Mall in Alberta, Canada, offers entertainment for the whole family at its Fantasyland Amusement Park. Teenagers in Greensburg, Pennsylvania, can hardly imagine what life was like before the video arcade opened at the Greengate Mall.

But, with all the changes, the shopping malls of today continue to serve the same dual function as "marketplaces" throughout history — places of commerce and social activity.

QUESTION CLAUSES

> Where's the train station?
> → Do you know **where the train station is**?
>
> Who should I ask for directions?
> → I wonder **who I should ask for directions**.
>
> How long does it take to get there?
> → Can you tell me **how long it takes to get there**?

Exercise 23

Example: What time does Paul's flight get in?
I don't remember **what time his flight gets in**.

1. Why can't the Nelsons come to the picnic?
   I wonder _why the N can't come to t. p._

2. What are they saying on the loudspeaker?
   Do you understand _what they are saying_

3. What kind of car did the Larsons buy?
   I don't know _what kind of car the L. bought_

4. When will they announce the election results?
   Everyone wants to know _when they'll announce t. e. r._

5. How long has Laura been studying German?
   Do you know _how long_? _Laura has been s. g._

6. Where's the nearest bus stop?
   Can you tell me _where's t.? nearest b. s._

7. Who did Mark Lipton marry?
   No one knows _who Mark L. married_

8. Why does Carl want to quit his job?
   I can't imagine _why Carl wants to quit_

Exercise 24

A. Fill in **more (... than)**, **less (... than)**, or **fewer (... than)**.

Example: Bill has 2 suitcases, and Jim has 1. Bill has **more** luggage **than** Jim does. Jim has **less**.

1. It usually takes us an hour to drive to Boston. Yesterday it took an hour and a half. There was __more__ traffic __than__ usual. There's usually __less__ traffic.

2. I had a lot of phone calls yesterday. Today I've only had one. I had __more__ calls yesterday __than__ today. I've had __fewer__ calls today.

3. Henry spent a half hour on the homework. Alice spent an hour. He spent __less__ time on it __than__ she did. She spent __more__ time.

4. The company used to have 5 branch offices. Now they have 20. They now have __more__ offices __than__ they used to. They used to have __fewer__.

B. Fill in **as much ... as** or **as many ... as**.

Example: I'll get **as much** work done **as** I can.

1. Al doesn't make __as much__ money __as__ he did at his former job.
2. Do you still go to __as many__ meetings __as__ you used to?
3. We don't have __as many__ computer workstations __as__ we need.
4. The doctor told Judy to get __as much__ exercise __as__ possible.
5. Not __as many__ people came to the party __as__ we expected.
6. Bill has had __as many__ opportunities __as__ his brother, but he hasn't done as well.

CHAPTER 7

WHERE *IS* THAT WAITER?

Janet Brown is having lunch with Bob Elliott and Paula Cramer at a new restaurant that has just opened up in the area.

Bob: Waiter, there must be some mistake. I ordered veal. I think this is chicken, isn't it?

Waiter: I'm sorry, sir, but that *is* veal.

Bob: It sure doesn't look like veal.

Waiter: Will there be anything else?

Paula: Not for me. ... Wait, on second thought, why don't you bring me a large glass of water?

Waiter: Yes, miss. Right away.

(The waiter leaves.)

Bob: I still say this tastes like chicken.

Janet: The salad isn't the greatest, either.

Paula: I know. It looks like it was left out overnight.

Bob: Who recommended this place anyway? It was you, Janet, wasn't it?

Janet: I confess. I'm the guilty one. But they just had their grand opening last week, and I thought we should give them a try.

Paula: You mean this place is brand-new?

Janet: Well, it's under new management. But it's been completely renovated since the new owners took over. It got a really nice write-up in last Sunday's paper.

Paula: Where *is* that waiter with my water, anyway?

Bob: If this is the kind of service they're going to be offering, they won't be around for long — that's for sure.

Paula: Ah, at last! Here comes the waiter!

Waiter: Here you are, miss. The tomato juice is for you, isn't it?

Trends in Restaurants

culture tip

According to statistics, people are "eating out" more often than ever before, but they're spending less time and money for each meal. For better or worse, the convenience of fast-food has become a way of life.

The character of the traditional full-service restaurant is changing as well. Here are a few of the new trends:

• friendly waiters and waitresses — Don't be surprised if you're greeted with a friendly "Hi, I'm Nick. I'll be your waiter this evening."

• salad bars — Your friendly waiter or waitress will often invite you to "visit the salad bar," where you can help yourself to a variety of vegetables, fruit, cheese, and the like.

• smoking sections — When you arrive at the restaurant or when you call to make a reservation, you may be asked if you prefer to sit in a smoking or non-smoking section.

Exercise 25

A. *Example:* They sell foreign newspapers at that newsstand.
Foreign newspapers are sold at that newsstand.

1. How do you spell your last name?
2. Someone will return your call this afternoon.
3. They didn't tell Richard about the meeting.
4. Where will they build the new hotel?
5. We send all packages via air mail.
6. Did the restaurant add a 15% tip to the bill?
7. Someone broke into Jim's apartment; they stole his stereo.
8. People don't usually drink red wine with chicken.
9. We don't pay the bills until the first of the month.
10. They didn't do the repair job right.

B. *Example:* Mrs. Drake saw the job applicants yesterday.
The job applicants were seen by Mrs. Drake yesterday.

1. Did the travel agent confirm your reservations?
2. Mr. Harper will give the presentation at today's meeting.
3. Did Mrs. Hunt teach Mary's French class last year?
4. Does the accounting department make out all the checks?
5. Japan exports a lot of electronic equipment.
6. Mark Twain wrote the book *Huckleberry Finn*.
7. A famous surgeon will operate on Mr. Taylor.
8. Thousands of people visit the museum every year.
9. A car hit the dog while it was crossing the street.
10. Bill's company doesn't hire people without college degrees.

TAG QUESTIONS

I'm not late for the meeting, **am I?**	No, you**'re not.** / Yes, you **are.**
You haven't eaten yet, **have you?**	No, I **haven't.** / Yes, I **have.**
They take credit cards, **don't they?**	Yes, they **do.** / No, they **don't.**
The service was excellent, **wasn't it?**	Yes, it **was.** / No, it **wasn't.**

Exercise 26

Example: You won't forget to call me, **_will you_** ?
No, **_I won't_** .

1. Bob would like to go to lunch with us, too, _____?
Yes, _____.

2. We've eaten at that restaurant before, _____?
Yes, _____.

3. I shouldn't be the one to make the decision, _____?
No, _____.

4. Barbara takes a vacation every July, _____?
Yes, _____.

5. Mr. Wilson has told everyone about the meeting, _____?
Yes, _____.

6. I'm not keeping you from anything, _____?
No, _____.

7. Nancy is going to explain the new filing system, _____?
Yes, _____.

8. You don't think it's going to rain, _____?
No, _____.

9. The Bakers went to Europe last year, _____?
Yes, _____.

10. The play doesn't start until 8, _____?
No, _____.

TO TIP OR NOT TO TIP?

It has been suggested that the word "tip" was first used in the English coffee houses of the 18th century. A box marked with the letters *T.I.P.* was put on the bar to encourage customers to pay in advance in order "**t**o **i**nsure **p**romptness."

Over the years, the custom of tipping has changed, and now tips are given *after* customers have been served, not before. So while a tip is intended to *reward* prompt service, it doesn't ensure it. The practice of tipping in restaurants varies from country to country, making it difficult for travelers to know when and how much to tip.

In the United States, it's customary to tip between 15% and 20% in restaurants, depending on the quality of service received. In Europe, however, a service charge is often included in the check, regardless of whether the customer is satisfied or not. It is acceptable to leave an additional 5% tip if the service was particularly good. In China and Japan, tipping is not widespread, and may even be considered an insult. So, the answer to the question "To tip or not to tip?" really depends a lot on where you are.

Exercise 27

Fill in the correct tense (active or passive) of the verb in parentheses.

Examples: Mrs. Barnes **has been teaching** at the university since 1980. *(teach)*

Her classes **are taken** by hundreds of students every year. *(take)*

1. Apparently the check I wrote last Monday *hasn't been cashed* yet. *(not cash)*
2. At about what time last night *did* the accident *been happen?* *(happen)*
3. Mr. Turner *was promoted* to department head last week. *(promote)*
4. Excuse me, I'm late for the conference. What room *will* it *been held* in? *(hold)*
5. *Was* Jim *working* on the schedule when you called him? *(work)*
6. These letters *won't be picked* until next Monday. *(not pick up)*
7. Patty's office is nearby, so she usually *walks* to work. *(walk)*
8. *Has* an effective cure for cancer *been found* yet? *(find)*
9. Your name *will be called* when the doctor is ready to see you. *(call)*
10. *Didn't* you and your wife *enjoy* the concert last night? *(not enjoy)*
11. Someone broke into Bill's car, but luckily nothing *was / had been taken*. *(take)*
12. Do you understand everything I *have said* so far? *(say)*
13. Right now several locations for the new offices *are being considered* *(consider)*
14. In some countries visas *aren't required*, just a valid passport. *(not require)*
15. Many flights *were delayed* yesterday because of bad weather. *(delay)*

Exercise 28

Example: Were you given a __written__ receipt when you had the T.V. repaired?

1. It was an _exciting_ race. Two of the runners were close until the finish.

2. We'll be _interested_ to hear how Jim likes his new job.

3. Was the customer _satisfied_ with the service he was given?

4. This has been an _exhausting_ day. I'm so tired I just want to go home and relax.

5. We finally found the restaurant, but the directions you gave us were _confusing_.

6. Sheila enjoyed the concert, but her husband thought it was _boring_.

7. Mr. Black gave an _interesting_ presentation at the sales meeting.

8. Have you ever had a _broken_ leg?

9. The actress was _unknown_ until she won the award. Now everyone recognizes her.

10. Having to admit a mistake can be an _embarrassing_ experience.

11. Was Bill's computer course _challenging_, or did he find it too easy?

12. I'm so _bored_ by all this rain. I wish it would stop.

- interesting
- boring
- confusing
- unknown
- exciting
- interested
- broken
- bored
- embarrassing
- exhausting
- **written**
- satisfied
- challenging

CHAPTER 8

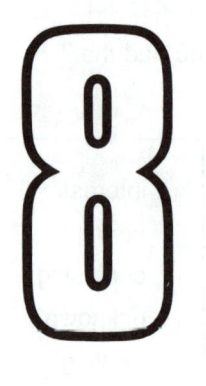

WHAT'S THE TROUBLE?

One day Janet noticed Bob Elliott in the parking lot in front of the office. He seemed to be having trouble starting his car.

Janet: Hey, Bob! What's the trouble?

Bob: Oh ... Hi, Janet. I don't know what's wrong. It's a brand-new car. I've only had it a month, and now it won't start.

Janet: I know a little about cars. Would you like me to take a look?

Bob: Oh, no. I don't want you to get yourself all dirty. I'll just call the garage and have them send a tow truck.

Janet: Come on, Bob, it won't take a minute. From the sound of it, I think I know just what the problem might be.

Bob: You're kidding! ... Well, O.K., if you insist. But be careful! Don't hurt yourself ...

Janet: I won't. Hmm ... this connection doesn't look right. Turn off the ignition, Bob. And don't try starting it till I tell you.

Bob: Listen, Janet, why don't I just have the garage come out and take a look at it? I've already checked everything. There's nothing you can do.

Janet: O.K., Bob, try it now.

Bob: It started! It actually started! What did you do?

Janet: It was a loose wire right here, near the distributor.

Bob: I don't believe it! Uh ... I was just going to check that myself!

Janet: I still think you should have a mechanic look at it. You may have to have a new wire put in.

Bob: Yeah, I'll check everything out as soon as I get home. You see ... I'm used to working on older cars. With these new ones, everything's been changed around.

Janet: They *are* complicated, that's for sure.

The Changing Role of Women

culture tip

The place of women in society has changed a lot over the years. In the above situation, we see Janet doing a job previously attempted only by men — repairing the car.

The image of women as primarily mothers and housewives is changing fast. Many women now have jobs outside the home, and the quality of their jobs is steadily improving: there are women working not only as nurses, teachers and waitresses, but also as doctors, lawyers, and business executives. However, many feel the progress has not been fast enough.

CAUSATIVES

I didn't look at the car *myself*.
→ I **had** a mechanic **look at** it.

have
let > someone **do** something
make

I didn't repair the car last week.
→ I **had** it **repaired** last week.

would like
want
get > something **done**
have

Exercise 29

Examples: We had the letter __*sent*__ special delivery. *(send)*

They made the thief __*tell*__ where the money was. *(tell)*

1. Did the Customs official make you _____ your suitcases? *(open)*

2. The Randalls don't let their children _____ past 9. *(stay up)*

3. Do you know a good place to get a radio _____? *(fix)*

4. Mr. Drake would like the reports _____ today. *(type)*

5. Your hair looks nice. Where did you have it _____? *(do)*

6. Mr. Morgan had Janet _____ his calls during the meeting. *(hold)*

7. We'd like to get the apartment _____ a different color. *(paint)*

8. The company always has a lawyer _____ the contracts. *(go over)*

9. We got new phones _____ last week. *(install)*

10. Why wouldn't Bill's boss let him _____ early? *(leave)*

Exercise 30

A. Fill in the correct reflexive pronoun.

Example: Be careful with that knife! You're going to cut **_yourself_**.

1. Did Janet really fix the car _____?
2. Thank you for inviting us. We've enjoyed _____.
3. The children would like to pick out their father's gift _____.
4. Do you really like the cake? I baked it _____.
5. Tell Bob to make _____ at home. I'll be off the phone in a minute.
6. What do you sometimes have to remind _____ to do?
7. Brad says he doesn't enjoy playing golf by _____.
8. The house _____ is nice, but the location isn't good.

B. Fill in **themselves** or **each other**.

Example: Sam and I haven't seen **_each other_** for years.

1. All of the guests helped _____ to dessert and coffee.
2. Dave and Maria have been avoiding _____ since they had their argument.
3. Can Joe and Ed move the sofa by _____, or would they like some help?
4. How long have Jim and Betty known _____?
5. The Turners have a good marriage, though they don't always agree with _____.
6. Those two kids can't look at _____ without laughing.
7. Don't worry. Patty and John can fix _____ some sandwiches.
8. How often do Gina and her sister write to _____?

ROLLS ROYCE GETS ROLLING

Henry Royce, a successful British businessman, was 40 years old when his doctor suggested that he slow down a little and try to take it easy. Royce thought a good way to do this would be to buy himself an automobile, which was still quite a novelty at the time. He ordered a 1901 French Decauville. But when the car finally arrived at the Manchester train station, it wouldn't start. The car had to be pushed all the way to Royce's home. It was then that Royce decided to build his own car — hardly what his doctor had in mind when he suggested a more relaxed lifestyle! Nevertheless, Royce, a self-taught engineer, spent the next year designing a two-cylinder vehicle.

In the meantime, a wealthy automobile enthusiast named Charles Rolls had set up a car dealership which sold mostly French and German cars. Rolls was a frequent competitor in automobile races sponsored by the Automobile Club of Great Britain, but always drove foreign-made cars. He had been looking around for a British car that could compete; and when a friend introduced him to Henry Royce, he knew the search was over. The 10-horsepower Royce automobile was reliable and had a very classic design. Rolls agreed to sell as many cars as Royce could produce. And in December of 1904, the first "Rolls Royce" automobiles made their debut.

Exercise 31

Example: You must cash this check immediately.
This check must be cashed immediately.

1. We should clean the house before the guests arrive.

2. They can repair the typewriter this afternoon.

3. Someone must stamp all the passports.

4. You have to sign these letters as soon as possible.

5. We shouldn't leave the car unlocked.

6. Someone must type this report before the meeting.

7. People shouldn't park cars in front of the driveway.

8. We don't have to make reservations more than a day in advance.

9. You may return the jacket if it doesn't fit.

10. They can't do the repair job in less than a day.

11. Someone should do the filing every morning.

12. You may not pay bills with a personal check.

13. You can reach Mr. Crawford at home in the evening.

14. They might not receive the package until Monday.

15. We'll have to replace these batteries.

Exercise 32

Fill in the correct phrasal verb from the box and supply the necessary pronoun.

Example: I don't remember Jeff's number. I'll have to **_look it up_** .

1. The blue jacket is nice. May I _____?

2. Mr. Spencer phoned while you were out. He'd like you to _____ .

3. I've finished typing the letters. Would you like to _____?

4. Bob called his wife from the airport and she went to _____ .

5. The picnic is scheduled for tomorrow, but we'll have to _____ if it rains.

6. The doctor was concerned about my smoking. He advised me to _____ .

| think over |
| call back |
| fill out |
| **look up** |
| make up |
| give up |
| call off |
| turn down |
| put away |
| look over |
| pick up |
| throw away |
| try on |

7. That radio is so loud! Would you please _____ a little?

8. Mary washed the dishes; Bobby dried them and _____ .

9. Here's your registration form. Please _____ and sign it.

10. I don't believe half of Sheila's stories. I think she _____ .

11. Those shoes are so worn out. Why don't you just _____?

12. They've made Phil a job offer, but he wants to _____ for a few days.

CHAPTER 9

YOU REALLY HAD QUITE A DAY!

Janet was on her way home from work one day when she ran into her friend Bill Sinclair.

Janet: Bill! Where did you get that black eye? And what are you doing here anyway? I thought you had already left for Vermont. When I saw you at work yesterday, you said you had already packed and were all set to go.

Bill: It's a long story. You see, the whole reason for my vacation was to get away and relax a little. I was even going to take the train, so I could enjoy the scenery on the way up. The trouble started this morning when my alarm clock didn't go off. By the time I got to the station, my train had already left. The next train wasn't due to leave for 12 hours, so I decided to rent a car instead.

Janet: That sounds like a good idea.

Bill: That's what *I* thought! But on my way to the car rental agency, I slipped and fell down some stairs in the subway.

Janet: So *that's* how you got the black eye!

Bill: I'm lucky I didn't kill myself. Anyway, when I fell, I broke my glasses and had to go all the way back home to pick up my other pair.

Janet: You really had quite a day!

Bill: And if you think it was easy lugging these suitcases all over town ... Anyway, when I finally got to the rental agency, the place was packed. After I had waited in line for half an hour and filled out all the forms, I realized I couldn't pay. It turned out I had left my wallet at home.

Janet: You sure have been through a lot! So what are you going to do now?

Bill: Well, for one thing, I've decided to forget about going to Vermont. I'm already a physical wreck, and I haven't even left town yet!

Knock on Wood!

Culture tip

It doesn't look like Bill had a very good day today. Who knows? Maybe he'll have better luck tomorrow. When things go well, we often say our luck is "good." Many people believe there are things we can do to bring us good luck and other things we can do to avoid bad luck.

Do you think twice before walking under a ladder? Does a little voice tell you not to open your umbrella inside the house? How do you feel if a black cat crosses in front of you? And, of course, there's that terrible number *13*. (Many buildings don't even dare to have a thirteenth floor!)

Thank goodness there are a few things we can do to improve our luck. We can carry a rabbit's foot, or hang a horseshoe over the door.

Well, let's hope our luck is better than Bill's. But, just to be sure, maybe we should "knock on wood."

THE PAST PERFECT

> David got to the station at 9:00. The train **left** at 8:45.
>
> When David got to the station, the train **had already left**.

Exercise 33

Examples: Fred arrived at 7:00. Bill ate dinner at 6:00. *(already)*
When Fred arrived, Bill had already eaten dinner.

I joined the company in 1985. Mr. Bates retired in 1986. *(not yet)*
When I joined the company, Mr. Bates hadn't retired yet.

1. We saw Paula on Tuesday. She returned from Paris Monday night. *(just)*
2. John got to the bank at 3:50. It closed at 4:00. *(not yet)*
3. Jill went home at 5:00. She didn't finish the report. *(still)*
4. Gary's letter came on Tuesday. I spoke to him on Monday. *(already)*
5. I went to the garage yesterday. They didn't fix my car till today. *(still)*
6. Ted phoned me at 9:05. I tried to call him at 9:00. *(just)*
7. The Bells got to the party at 7:30. Dinner was served at 8:00. *(not yet)*
8. Mrs. Drake asked for the report at noon. We finished it at 11:30. *(already)*
9. I finished breakfast at 7:00. Tommy didn't leave for school till 8:00. *(still)*
10. Mary finished school in 1979. She met her husband in 1981. *(not yet)*

Exercise 34

Example: (had ... gone / have ... gone)
I **had** just **gone** to bed when the phone rang.

1. (wasn't writing / hadn't written) *hadn't written*
   I finally called Sue because she _____ for such a long time.

2. (have ... learned / did ... learn)
   Where *did* you *learn* to speak English so well?

3. (haven't received / hadn't received) *hadn't received*
   The package was sent a week ago, but we _____ it yet.

4. (had left / was leaving) *was leaving*
   Ellen and Jeff ran to the bus stop because the bus _____.

5. (didn't ... make / hadn't ... made)
   Why *didn't* Mr. Evans *make* it to the meeting last Friday?

6. (Did ... eat / Had ... eaten)
   Had you ever *eaten* Indian food before last night?

7. (has been snowing / had been snowing)
   It _____ since early this morning. *has been snowing*

8. (had ... been waiting / has ... been waiting)
   How long *had* Mary *been* *w.* for Ed when he finally showed up?

9. (wasn't feeling / hasn't been feeling) *wasn't feel-*
   Bert went home from work early because he _____ well.

10. (hadn't ... flown / didn't ... fly) *hadn't flown*
    Lisa was excited about the trip because she _____ ever _____ before.

11. (Has ... left / Had ... left)
    Had Mr. Palmer already *left* when you got to the office?

12. (had ... stayed / did ... stay)
    What hotel *did* Al *stay* at when he was in London?

BETTER SAFE THAN SORRY

When you get up in the morning, you probably don't think much about all the dangers you face even before you leave the house. When people think of getting hurt, the first thing that comes to mind is a car or plane accident. The truth is, however, that millions of people suffer serious injuries, and even death, in their own homes.

As you walk downstairs, consider that falls (especially on stairs) account for 30% of all accidental deaths in the home. And be very careful as you plug in the toaster: many people die from electrocution due to bad electrical wiring. In fact, you should think twice before biting into that piece of toast, because statistics indicate that thousands of people die each year as a result of choking on food.

With all these hidden dangers, you might think that it would be safer just to stay in bed. Well, think again. A surprising number of people are injured while in, or around, a bed. And, as we all know, *that* is precisely where most people die. So, you might as well take your chances and get out of bed — before you fall out!

Exercise 35

Example: Don't buy the stereo __b__ you get a good price.
a. when
b. unless

1. We didn't watch the movie __b__ we had already seen it.
   a. until
   b. since

2. __b__ Joe studied the words, there are some he doesn't remember.
   a. So
   b. Although

3. I've applied for a transfer __a__ my boss has approved it.
   a. and
   b. as soon as

4. Was the product heavily advertised __a__ it was first introduced?
   a. while
   b. when

5. The Halls stayed an extra day in Berlin __b__ they could look up some friends.
   a. because
   b. so

6. Maria didn't wake up __a__ her alarm went off at 6:00.
   a. until
   b. since

7. Did you call Fred __a__ you heard the news about his brother?
   a. as soon as
   b. until

8. It was raining, __b__ the children wanted to play outside anyway.
   a. although
   b. but

9. Janet left the message on Mr. Morgan's desk, __b__ she's sure he got it.
   a. but
   b. so

10. Sales have fallen __a__ foreign competition has gotten stronger.
    a. because
    b. so

11. Mr. Baker hadn't thought about buying a computer __b__ his friend got one.
    a. and
    b. until

12. Did Paul learn to speak Japanese __a__ he was living in Tokyo?
    a. while
    b. until

WORD FAMILIES

> **accident:** Mr. Bell had a car **accident** on the way to the airport.
> **accidental:** Their meeting in the street was **accidental**.
> **accidentally:** Ted **accidentally** knocked over the glass of water.

Exercise 36

Fill in the correct form of the word in bold face.

Example: The sign said "**Danger!** Do Not Enter," but we couldn't find out why the area was ___dangerous___.

1. Jane's company has a big **advertising** budget. They _____ in many newspapers and magazines.

2. Mark **competes** in a lot of races. He's in at least five _____ a year.

3. The factory is trying to increase **production**. They want to _____ 20% more than last year.

4. Marilyn's boss wasn't **satisfied** with the report. He said the figures weren't _____.

5. John **inherited** $20,000 from his aunt. He used his _____ to buy a sailboat.

6. Larry is interested in **science** and math. He wants to be a _____ when he grows up.

7. We often go to the movies for **entertainment**. Comedies are especially _____.

8. Mr. Parker is very **decisive**. He's used to making important _____ quickly.

9. Bill **suggested** that we try the Roma Restaurant. It was a good _____; the food was excellent.

10. Our office is in the **center** of town. It was chosen for its _____ location.

CHAPTER 10

AN INVITATION

Susan Morgan and her husband, John, are relaxing in their living room after dinner.

Susan: Oh, John, I forgot to tell you — Linda Stamford called a couple of days ago. She said Ed had just gotten a big promotion.

John: But he hasn't been with that company very long, has he? Didn't he just start there about six months ago?

Susan: That's right. Apparently, it all started about a month ago when Ed got a terrific job offer from a company in Texas. Linda said he'd almost decided to accept the job when his company heard about the offer and gave him a big promotion ... with a much higher salary! They even promised him a company car as part of the deal.

John: So what did he decide to do?

Susan: He decided to stay where he is. Now he wants to throw a party to celebrate, and Linda called to invite us. She told me she'd already invited about twenty people.

John: When is it?

Susan: This Saturday night.

John: Hmm ... they're not giving us much notice. And didn't you tell me last week that you'd gotten theater tickets for Saturday night?

Susan: Oh, that's right! I'd forgotten all about it. Well ... what do you think we should do, go to the party or see the play?

John: I'd rather go to the party. Why don't we give the theater tickets to the Randalls?

Susan: We can't. They've been invited to the party, too!

John: I know. I'll give them to my secretary, Janet. I think she has a new boyfriend.

You're Invited

culture tip

Because they know each other well, Susan may get in touch with Linda a few days before the party to ask if there's anything she can bring, like a special dessert or some snacks.

However, when we're invited to dinner in a foreign country, it's not always that clear. We're often left wondering — what time should we arrive and what should we bring? In many English-speaking countries most parties begin around 8:00 — except for dinner parties, which usually start around 6:30 or 7:00. It's always a good idea to bring a small gift for your hosts: a bottle of wine, a box of chocolates, or perhaps some flowers.

And remember, American punctuality in business carries over to social functions. If the party invitation is for 7:00, it's best not to arrive more than 15 minutes late.

REPORTED SPEECH — STATEMENTS

> Linda said, "Ed **got** a promotion."
> → She told me he **had gotten** a promotion.
>
> Linda said, "I**'m inviting** 20 people to the party."
> → She said she **was inviting** 20 people to the party.
>
> Linda said, "Dinner **will be served** at 7."
> → She told her guests dinner **would be served** at 7.

Exercise 37

Example: "I've just moved to a larger apartment."
Betty told Jack __she had just moved to a larger apartment__.

1. "I forgot my wallet at home."
   David said _I had forgotten_

2. "Mr. Nelson's office is on the 12th floor."
   The woman at the desk told me _Mr. N.'s office was_

3. "I'll have the T.V. fixed as soon as possible."
   The repairman said _he would have_

4. "I went to a concert over the weekend."
   Tom told us _had gone_

5. "The plane will take off on time."
   The airline told us _would take_

6. "We haven't been notified about the meeting."
   Gary and Joe said _had been_

7. "I'll have a table for you in a few minutes."
   The waitress told us _would have_

8. "My brother doesn't live in Chicago anymore."
   Paul said _didn't live_

9. "We won't be able to come to the party."
   The Millers told Linda _would not be able_

10. "I can't get you a reservation for the 21st."
    The travel agent told me _couldn't get_

WOULD RATHER • HAD BETTER

> Susan prefers to go to the party.
> → She **would rather** go to the party.
> → She**'d rather not** use the theater tickets.
>
> We should get to the airport early.
> → We **had better** get there early.
> → We**'d better not** get there late.

Exercise 38

Fill in **would rather (not)** or **had better (not)**.

Example: Gary has gotten to work late twice this week.
He **'d better not** be late again.

1. It's raining hard. We _d better_ take a taxi back to the hotel.
2. John _____ spend his vacation at home than travel.
3. Where _____ you _____ live, in a big city or a small town?
4. Laura _____ forget to call Mr. Rogers before she leaves.
5. The Millers have the money, but they _____ pay that much for a car.
6. That restaurant is always crowded; we _____ make reservations.
7. We'd like to go to the beach, but our children _____ see Disneyland.
8. You _____ park there, or you'll get a ticket.
9. They _____ fix that road. It's dangerous!
10. _____ you _____ go to the movies tonight or tomorrow night?
11. I can take my car if Jim _____ drive in the snow.
12. The kids _____ be watching T.V. They're supposed to be in bed!

MAKING "SMALL TALK"

One of the most important skills needed to feel comfortable at large parties is how to make "small talk" — those small, almost meaningless bits of conversation that come up over and over on social occasions.

Of course, the weather is an ideal topic. Everyone has an opinion about it, and it's not controversial. Another good topic is traffic and transportation. You can always ask someone how he or she got to the party, what route they took, how much traffic there was, and how good the host's directions were. This topic can then be expanded into a general discussion of traffic in the city, new modes of transportation, and so on.

Another frequent topic is the decor of the place where the party is being held. The tables and walls of most homes or apartments are filled with dozens of little knick-knacks that can be looked at, examined, and discussed.

The subject of what a person does for a living invariably comes up. In many cases a person's occupation is simple to express: "I'm an accountant." Other occupations are more difficult to describe and you may need to have the person explain what he meant when he said he was a "computer systems analyst." Depending on how much time you have to kill, you may end up knowing more about the person than you really want to!

Exercise 39

Examples: "Are you having a good time?" the hostess asked us.
The hostess asked us if we were having a good time.

The man asked Jim, "Where do you work?"
The man asked him where he worked.

1. Carol asked me, "How long will you be staying in London?"

2. "Has Janet come back from lunch yet?" Bob asked John.

3. Sheila asked the repairman, "When can I pick up my radio?"

4. "Did you complain to the manager?" I asked my husband.

5. Mrs. Hall called to ask, "How late is the store open?"

6. "Will Joe have time to read the memo before the meeting?" I asked Anne.

7. "Does Linda need any help decorating for the party?" my friend asked.

8. "How many people were invited to the wedding reception?" asked Jill.

9. "Have all the sales figures been turned in?" Mr. Morgan asked.

10. The operator asked Ken, "Did you dial the number correctly?"

11. Tom asked me, "When did you get back from Tokyo?"

12. "Can you come to dinner next Saturday?" Mrs. Adams asked us.

13. Patty asked Ted, "Why didn't you go to the meeting?"

14. "How long have you been waiting for me?" my wife asked me.

15. "When was Mr. Butler transferred to Chicago?" I asked.

Exercise 40

Examples: Sue had a dress __made__ when she was in Hong Kong. *(make)*
She wanted the tailor __to finish__ it while she was there. *(finish)*
He couldn't, so she had him __send__ it to her. *(send)*

1. What address would you like the flowers _____ to? *(deliver)*
2. Please have Mr. Spencer _____ me as soon as he gets in. *(call)*
3. How did you get the children _____ their homework so fast? *(do)*
4. Will the doctor make Albert _____ smoking? *(quit)*
5. The Tuckers haven't had their house _____ for several years. *(paint)*
6. Who can we get _____ the plants while we're gone? *(water)*
7. Why haven't they gotten the copy machine _____ yet? *(fix)*
8. They've asked Frank _____ at the annual sales banquet. *(speak)*
9. The flight attendant wouldn't let us _____ our seats. *(change)*
10. Joe said he didn't want the meeting _____ in his office. *(hold)*
11. Where would you like the delivery man _____ these boxes? *(put)*
12. Mr. Brown didn't want his wife _____ a birthday party for him. *(have)*
13. Does the law require citizens _____ identification? *(carry)*
14. Julie said she'd like her messages _____ with the secretary. *(leave)*
15. Why did Bill ask us _____ his plans a secret? *(keep)*

CHAPTER 11

CONGRATULATIONS!

Kevin Williams, manager of Superior Products' London office, is meeting with John Morgan in New York.

John: So, Kevin, that's the situation. After three years of trying to establish a foothold in Europe, the results are still disappointing. To tell you the truth, we've actually considered closing down the European operation altogether.

Kevin: Closing down? I didn't realize the situation was *that* serious. In London, we've been rather optimistic.

John: I can understand that. Your office is the only one that's shown an increase in sales ... and profits.

Kevin: Yes, but remember — it took us three years to do it. If I were you, John, I would give the other managers a little more time. I'm sure they can show positive results, too.

John: I'm not so sure, Kevin. Look ... we've invested an enormous amount of money in these operations, and we don't have much to show for it. But in your case, we've seen steady results right from the start.

Kevin: Well, we *have* been quite successful so far. I'm not really that familiar with the other operations. Each country is really quite different. Each one has its own set of problems.

John: But they all need one thing — energetic leadership. That's been the key to *your* success. I'm convinced of it! I'm not sure the other managers are as much on top of their operations as they could be.

Kevin: Well, I suppose that's possible, but ...

John: No "but's" about it. We have a problem. But we may also have a solution. Kevin, I need someone who can take charge of the entire European operation — someone with a lot of experience, and someone with a successful track record. How does the title *Vice President — European Operations* sound to you?

Kevin: Vice President?

John: You've earned it, Kevin. Congratulations!

Kevin: Thanks, John. I hope I won't disappoint you.

It Pays to Switch

culture tip

We don't know from the conversation how long Kevin has been with his company or how satisfied he is with his job, but the promotion should be an incentive for him to stay with his present firm.

Statistics, however, show that employees who stay with the same company for their entire working career are becoming the exception rather than the rule. This trend is especially widespread in the United States, where it has become almost a status symbol for people to be able to say they've worked for several different companies. Besides, they often find it financially rewarding to switch companies rather than wait for their own company to give them a big raise or a good promotion.

In other countries, more emphasis is placed on longer tenure and company loyalty. Employees expect to stay with the same company for all or most of their working career.

Exercise 41

A. *Example:* Paul enjoys music. He goes to a lot of concerts.
If he **_didn't enjoy_** it, he **_wouldn't go_** to a lot of concerts.

1. Fred has to work until midnight. He's tired in the morning.
If he _____ work until midnight, he _____ tired in the morning.

2. I'm hungry in the morning. I eat a big breakfast.
If I _____ hungry, I _____ a big breakfast.

3. Janet plays tennis every day. She lives near the courts.
She _____ tennis every day if she _____ near the courts.

4. Mr. Bell is tied up with a client. He has to postpone the meeting.
If he _____, he _____ postpone it.

5. The plant runs efficiently. It has modern equipment.
It _____ efficiently if it _____ modern equipment.

B. *Examples:* We don't have time. We can't go to the museum.
If we **_had_** time, we **_could go_** to the museum.

My car doesn't run smoothly. It isn't tuned up.
It **_would run_** smoothly if it **_were_** tuned up.

1. Jill can't take a vacation this year. She doesn't have enough money.
She _____ a vacation if she _____ enough money.

2. I'm not you. I won't see a doctor about those headaches.
If I _____ you, I _____ a doctor about those headaches.

3. We won't get the report done today. Karen can't help us.
We _____ it _____ today if she _____ us.

4. Mark doesn't exercise regularly. He's not in good shape.
If he _____ regularly, he _____ in good shape.

5. Robert doesn't live near the office. He can't walk to work.
If he _____ near the office, he _____ to work.

HOPE • THINK • GUESS

> Did Mrs. Harvey get to the meeting on time?
> – **I hope so.**
> – **I hope she got to the meeting on time.**
>
> Where's David? Isn't he coming with us?
> – **I guess not.**
> – **I guess he isn't coming with us.**

Exercise 42 X

Examples: It's not supposed to rain today, is it? *(think)*
I don't think so.
I don't think it's supposed to rain today.

1. John doesn't have to work late again tonight, does he? *(hope)*

2. Bill doesn't answer his phone. Isn't he at home? *(guess)*

3. Can Laura give us a ride to the train station? *(hope)*

4. Mr. Parker didn't make a mistake in his calculations, did he? *(think)*

5. Should Mrs. Drake sign these letters before she leaves? *(guess)*

6. We won't have to wait long for a table, will we? *(hope)*

7. They discussed the contract at the meeting, didn't they? *(think)*

8. The letters are still here. Hasn't the mail been picked up? *(guess)*

9. You don't have to see the dentist again, do you? *(hope)*

10. We won't have any trouble finding a hotel, will we? *(think)*

ARE YOU A "WORKAHOLIC"?

Most people are aware of how serious an addiction to alcohol or cigarettes can be, but there is one addiction that is often ignored until it's too late: an addiction to *work*. "Workaholics" are so addicted to their jobs that work has become an obsession. Are you a workaholic? Ask yourself these questions:

- Do you arrive at the office early and leave late?
- Do you work extra hours on weekends?
- Do you make it a point to bring work home with you?
- Is it difficult for you to sleep because of job-related matters?
- Do your family and friends complain that your job means more to you than they do?
- Do you work such long hours that you have no time for activities that are not job-related?

If more than three of these symptoms apply to you, you *may* be a workaholic. Now — think about taking a vacation! If the very idea horrifies you, you have a problem. It's not an easy one to solve and not one to be taken lightly, either. Your best course of action might be to take that vacation and prove to yourself that there *is* life outside the office. You might just find that you actually enjoy it!

Exercise 43

Examples: We got to the airport early. It was necessary.
It was necessary for us to get to the airport early.
Jim can't finish the report today. Why isn't it possible?
Why isn't it possible for him to finish the report today?

1. Theresa learned to use the word processor. It was hard.

2. We paid the bill before it was due. Was it a good idea?

3. The company didn't raise its prices. It wasn't necessary.

4. I'd like to have next Tuesday off. Would it be possible?

5. Mr. Spencer attended the meeting, too. It was better.

6. Mrs. Tucker knew the details of the contract. Why was it so important?

7. Brad didn't accept the job offer. It was impossible.

8. The Boston plant might not meet its quota. It will be difficult.

9. The salesmen must be familiar with the products. Why is it important?

10. You should call the personnel office today. It would be better.

11. The Blakes made reservations. It was a good idea.

12. We can't get hold of Paul during the day. It's impossible.

SUCH • SO

> It was **such a good play** *(that)* we'd like to see it again.
> It was **so good** *(that)* we'd like to see it again.
>
> The Williams like Miami because it has **such nice weather**.
> They like Miami because the weather is **so nice**.
>
> Tom is **such a hard worker** *(that)* he deserves a raise.
> He works **so hard** *(that)* he deserves a raise.

Exercise 44

Fill in **such** or **so**.

Example: This is _such_ a delicious cake! May I have another piece?

1. Eric liked Brazil because the people there were _____ friendly.

2. Mr. Bentley is _____ a rich man he has houses all over the world.

3. Was the weather _____ bad that you couldn't go out?

4. I've always liked that restaurant because it has _____ good seafood.

5. Why has your department been working _____ long hours lately?

6. It was _____ windy yesterday that my umbrella turned inside out.

7. Everyone respects Jeff because he's _____ an honest person.

8. My steak was _____ tough I could hardly cut it!

9. Where did Janice learn to play the guitar _____ well?

10. If it weren't _____ a cool day, we'd go to the beach.

11. Were you surprised that _____ many people came to the meeting?

12. I've never understood why Mr. Grant is _____ a successful businessman.

CHAPTER 12

I WON'T BE A MINUTE

Kevin Williams and his wife, Sarah, have ended their stay in New York and are returning to London. Right now, they're at the airline ticket counter at JFK Airport in New York.

... Trans National Airlines Flight 915 to Rome is now boarding at Gate 22. All passengers please proceed to Gate 22.

Attendant: Yes ... may I help you?

Kevin: We'd like to check in for Flight 807 to London.

Attendant: May I see your tickets and passports, please? ... Thank you. How many bags do you have?

Kevin: Three suitcases, plus these two flight bags. It's a good thing we bought the second flight bag, Sarah. If we didn't have it, there wouldn't be enough room for all the presents and souvenirs.

Sarah: We *did* get a lot, didn't we?

Kevin: Oh, well, we picked up some really nice things, and some good bargains, too.

Attendant: Would you prefer a smoking or non-smoking section?

Kevin: Non-smoking, please. Oh, and we'd like a window seat, if possible.

Attendant: Certainly. Here are your boarding passes and your baggage claim tickets. Your flight will be boarding in about 30 minutes.

Kevin: Thank you. ... Well, what shall we do now? I'm rather hungry myself.

Sarah: I am, too. We haven't had a bite to eat since lunch.

Kevin: Hmm ... if our flight weren't leaving so soon, we could have a snack in that restaurant over there. Oh, well, it doesn't matter. We'll be having dinner on the plane in a little while anyway.

Sarah: You're right. But I would like to get something to read. Do you think there's time for me to run back to the newsstand and get a magazine?

Kevin: I think so. But I wouldn't take too long if I were you. Remember, the next flight doesn't leave till tomorrow afternoon!

Sarah: Don't worry. I won't be a minute. I'm not too anxious to spend the night here at the airport!

Thanks for Not Smoking

culture tip

We've all heard the question "Smoking or non-smoking?" when making plane reservations. And when we travel by train, we have to choose whether we want to sit in a smoking or non-smoking car. In many countries these choices may not be available much longer. In the United States smoking is now prohibited in most public buildings and on several airlines. And the smoking car on trains is already becoming a thing of the past.

The "smoking / non-smoking" question is now being asked in places it was never heard before. Restaurants are designating separate sections for smokers, hotels are assigning special rooms, and many companies now provide separate areas for employees who smoke. And, of course, we are all bombarded daily with anti-smoking messages in the newspapers, on the radio, and on television.

But the strongest deterrent to smoking may be social pressure — the subtle looks of displeasure as a smoker lights up and the social isolation as his circle of friends narrows to the few remaining smokers.

Exercise 45

Fill in the correct tense (active or passive) of the verb in parentheses.

Examples: Jim **met** many nice people when he lived in London. (meet)
   Everything **will be explained** at tomorrow's meeting. (explain)

1. Say hello to Paul the next time you _____ him. (see)

2. Janet _____ at 8:15, and her boss _____ a few minutes after she did. (arrive / come in)

3. How long _____ you _____ about the company's plans for expansion? (know)

4. We _____ for 15 minutes, and the waiter _____ even _____ our order yet! (wait / not take)

5. Go ahead and turn off the T.V. I _____ it. (not watch)

6. The Blakes _____ of the hotel after they finish packing. (check out)

7. Last year, Brad _____ travel on business at all; but so far this year, he _____ three trips. (not have to / make)

8. _____ the Blakes usually _____ to dinner Sundays? (go out)

9. We _____ the car tuned up last week, but it _____ still _____ a strange noise. (have / make)

10. _____ the children _____ outside when it started to rain? (play)

11. They say the new airport _____ for 5 years. (not finish)

12. The mail _____ by the time I finished the letter. (pick up)

13. Fish should _____ when it's fresh. (eat)

14. We enjoyed Paris. We _____ never _____ there before. (be)

15. You _____ the bus if you _____. (not catch / not hurry)

TIME EXPRESSIONS

in	for	since	at	during
on	ago	until	by	now

Exercise 46

Fill in the correct time expressions from the box above.

Example: I won't be ready to leave **for** a few minutes yet.

1. Mr. Palmer is busy now, but he'll be free _____ about 20 minutes.
2. Would you ask John to please wait _____ I get to the office?
3. That product was taken off the market several years _____.
4. When Bill was in school, he worked _____ the day and took classes _____ night.
5. Have the Taylors lived in the neighborhood _____ a long time?
6. The conference will begin _____ Friday _____ 8:30 a.m.
7. Have you been to the Roma Restaurant _____ it was remodeled?
8. Jane said nearly everyone had left _____ the time she got to the party.
9. Last year my parents visited me _____ three weeks.
10. Mr. Baker hasn't been well _____ his operation.
11. Jim was annoyed because people were whispering _____ the movie.
12. Kate's exam was easy. She finished it _____ less than an hour.
13. Your report isn't due _____ Tuesday, but you'd better get started on it _____.
14. Did Martin tell you he'd be arriving _____ Wednesday morning?
15. The travel agent said we should be at the airport _____ 3:30 _____ the latest.

COME FLY WITH ME!

The first flight attendants were hired in 1922 by British Daimler Airways. They were teenage boys who wore uniforms like the ones worn by hotel bellboys. Since neither food nor beverages were served, these first flight "stewards" didn't really provide much actual service. Their main function was to give passengers a sense of comfort.

In 1930, United Air Lines decided to hire women as "stewardesses." The women were all registered nurses, and their nursing skills often came in handy since so many passengers became airsick in those early days of air travel. The airline believed that passengers would feel even safer if the stewardesses wore their white nurses' uniforms.

In addition to serving meals, stewardesses offered passengers cotton to muffle the noise of the engines. In those days, being a stewardess wasn't considered a glamorous job, and the women were sometimes called upon to help carry luggage on board ... and even fuel the plane! But the most crucial duty of the first stewardesses was to make sure that passengers didn't confuse the lavatory door with the emergency exit, which was just next to it!

Exercise 47

Examples: (*feels / would feel / will feel*)
The doctor said Ed **would feel** better if he got more exercise.

(*go / will go / went*)
If we **go** to Italy this year, we'll spend a week in Rome.

1. (*gets / will get / got*)
   Mr. Butler will sign the letters as soon as he _____ back.

2. (*Will ... take / Would ... take / Did ... take*)
   _____ you _____ the train to Paris if you had more time?

3. (*am / would be / were*)
   If I _____ you, I'd get to the airport at least an hour before the flight.

4. (*would ... reach / can ... reach / did ... reach*)
   Where _____ we _____ you if something happens?

5. (*wouldn't leave / didn't leave / won't leave*)
   Mr. Gordon _____ until he finishes his work.

6. (*checked / will check / would check*)
   The Williams _____ their luggage before they get something to eat.

7. (*will offer / offered / offer*)
   Would Paul take the job if they _____ it to him?

8. (*won't be / weren't / isn't*)
   If the weather _____ good, the plane won't take off on time.

9. (*arrive / will arrive / would arrive*)
   I'll call you when I _____ at my hotel in London.

10. (*won't drive / wouldn't drive / doesn't drive*)
    Jane _____ to work if she lived closer to the subway line.

11. (*will ... do / would ... do / did ... do*)
    What _____ we _____ if we miss our connection?

12. (*can't afford / couldn't afford / won't be able to afford*)
    Bill _____ school if he didn't have a part-time job.

Exercise 48

Arrange the following words into sentences. Add the necessary punctuation.

Examples: are / to / vacation / go / on / planning / you / when
When are you planning to go on vacation?

hope / have / time / I / that / good / you / a
I hope that you have a good time.

1. on vacation / to / are / Florida / going / Cheryl and Mike

2. was / their / said / a nice / Florida / friends / place / that / for a vacation

3. a good hotel / they / make / a travel agent / reservations / had / at

4. too / their / made / were / travel agent / the / plane reservations / by

5. the / should / great / this / be / time / weather / of year

6. two / they / spend / days / to / at / want / Disneyworld / at least

7. everything / couldn't / they / the travel agent / them / see / told / in one day

8. looking forward / been / the trip / for / they've / to / months

9. their / bags / already / they've / packed

10. it sounds / doesn't / a / it / great / like / vacation

ANSWER KEY

Exercise 1   1. b 2. b 3. a 4. b 5. a 6. a 7. a 8. a

Exercise 2   1. rarely rings 2. 'm *(= I am)* usually 3. Does ... ever see 4. are generally 5. often visit 6. sometimes takes 7. don't ever watch 8. Is ... always 9. doesn't often arrive 10. are never 11. seldom takes 12. never snows 13. do ... usually have 14. sometimes go 15. is rarely

Exercise 3   1. they haven't bought him a car yet 2. he's *(= he is)* bringing you the wine 3. I left her a message 4. you've *(= you have)* shown me the memo 5. she's *(= she is)* not serving them coffee 6. he'd *(= he would)* like to sell him a car 7. he didn't give me his phone number 8. she'll *(= she will)* mail us her pictures 9. he offered him the job 10. she hasn't written her a letter lately

Exercise 4   1. Yes, we're *(= we are)* still supposed to have a meeting next Friday. 2. Yes, he's *(= he is)* still out of town on business. 3. No, I don't play tennis anymore. 4. Yes, he was still busy with a client when I called. 5. No, he doesn't smoke anymore. 6. No, they don't have to work on Saturdays anymore. 7. No, when I met her, she wasn't working at the bank anymore. 8. Yes, I'm *(= I am)* still waiting to see her. 9. Yes, they were still by the door when I left. 10. No, it doesn't stop at the corner of 17th and Elm anymore. 11. Yes, she was still thinking about changing jobs when I saw her. 12. No, we don't keep in touch anymore.

Exercise 5   can't, May, must, Can, can't, should, shouldn't, can't, can't

Exercise 6   1. must 2. may not 3. could 4. may not 5. must 6. could 7. shouldn't 8. might 9. might not 10. must not

Exercise 7   A) 1. any 2. a lot 3. any, some 4. some 5. some, any 6. any 7. no 8. a lot

B) 1. a little, much 2. much 3. a few 4. many 5. many 6. many, a few 7. a little 8. much

Exercise 8   A) 1. They want to move to London, but they can't do it this year. 2. She can swim, but she doesn't like to swim

Exercise 8 (cont'd.)

in the ocean. 3. We should make reservations, but we don't have to make them a month in advance. 4. I must leave soon, but I don't have to leave right now. 5. He likes to drive fast, but he shouldn't. 6. She should work on the report, but she doesn't want to do it now. 7. I should go to the meeting, but I don't have to. 8. He likes to play football, but he can't play this Sunday.

B) 1. Would 2. does 3. do 4. would 5. would 6. Do 7. would 8. Does

Exercise 9

... **took** a shower, **shaved**, and **got dressed**; then he **had** breakfast. He **didn't eat** much — just toast, juice, and coffee. He **left** the house about 7:45 and **caught** the 8 o'clock train. His secretary, Janet, **came** in earlier than he **did**; so when he **got** there, she **was** already at her desk. She **opened** the mail and **brought** it to him, and **gave** him his messages. He **was** very busy — he **made** a lot of phone calls and **saw** several clients. After lunch, he **wrote** a few memos and **gave** them to Janet to type. He **met** with his marketing director and then **read** the latest sales reports. At 5:00, he **said** good night to Janet and **went** home. On the way home, he **stopped** to buy the evening paper. He and his wife **didn't have** dinner until 7:00, so he **had** time to sit down and watch the news. After a long day at the office, he **felt** like relaxing.

Exercise 10

1. He should, too. 2. She doesn't, either. 3. We weren't, either. 4. Rome does, too. 5. His did, too. 6. They do, too. 7. She shouldn't, either. 8. They are, too. 9. He can, too. 10. His won't, either. 11. I didn't, either. 12. She did, too. 13. They are, too. 14. She doesn't, either. 15. They weren't, either.

Exercise 11

1. his, mine 2. Our, yours 3. her, his 4. hers 5. theirs 6. his, ours 7. their 8. their, his 9. your, mine 10. his 11. my, his 12. Your, mine

Exercise 12

1. arrives 2. Does ... work 3. found 4. doesn't get 5. Were ... able to 6. spoke, gave 7. taught 8. broke, couldn't walk 9. did ... get back 10. Does ... take 11.

Exercise 12 (cont'd.)	don't drink, keeps 12. did ... open 13. lost 14. did ... do 15. does ... meet
Exercise 13	1. haven't made 2. Has ... heard from 3. has ... taught 4. has ... given 5. has ... been 6. have looked at, haven't bought 7. Have ... eaten 8. 've *(= we have)* had 9. hasn't gotten 10. haven't ... stopped by 11. has done 12. Hasn't ... told
Exercise 14	1. yet 2. since 3. since 4. already 5. for 6. already 7. yet 8. since 9. for 10. yet 11. already, yet 12. since 13. for 14. already 15. since
Exercise 15	1. Has ... made 2. was, didn't ring 3. did ... quit 4. don't live 5. has ... won 6. reads 7. meant, forgot 8. haven't seen, got 9. doesn't deliver 10. Did ... learn, lived 11. have ... understood, works 12. does ... see 13. hasn't rained 14. Do ... play 15. retired, hasn't replaced
Exercise 16	1. the coldest 2. faster 3. more valuable than 4. farther 5. as heavy as 6. the most exciting 7. more challenging than 8. better 9. the wealthiest 10. as well as 11. the best 12. as difficult as
Exercise 17	1. How soon is it going to close? 2. What time does she have to get up tomorrow morning? 3. Where are we going to stay? 4. How long will he be out of town? 5. When is he taking her out to dinner? 6. How much will it cost to get the T.V. repaired? 7. When does your French class begin? 8. Which train are they taking? 9. Where's *(= where is)* she going to meet us? 10. Why won't you have time to finish the report? 11. What time does his plane get in? 12. Whose typewriter is he going to borrow?
Exercise 18	1. leaves, 'll *(= will)* meet 2. will ... wear, goes out 3. will miss, doesn't get on 4. gets, 'll *(= will)* order 5. finishes, 'll *(= will)* look for 6. doesn't come, 'll *(= will)*come 7. change, will ... charge 8. opens, won't have 9. will call, arrives 10. wait, won't be

Exercise 19   A) 1. too small 2. large enough 3. old enough 4. too dark 5. wide enough 6. too crowded

B) 1. too much 2. enough 3. too much 4. too many 5. enough 6. too many

Exercise 20   A) 1. going, flying 2. to hear about 3. Smoking 4. waiting 5. to make 6. Knowing

B) 1. We had dinner before going to the movies. 2. Janet got a raise by working very hard. 3. You can't learn a second language without having to study. 4. I'm looking forward to seeing you next week. 5. Billy got sick from eating too much candy. 6. Tom apologized for leaving early. 7. Janet's all excited about starting her new job next week. 8. Kevin is proud of being a top student in his class. 9. The Whites have talked about buying a bigger house. 10. We'll have a glass of wine after ordering dinner.

Exercise 21   1. was ... going, saw 2. talked, was thinking about 3. Did ... have, were attending 4. went off, were taking 5. Was ... snowing, got up 6. ran into, was walking 7. wasn't watching, had 8. didn't want to, were having 9. rang, was taking 10. kept, was landing 11. borrowed, was using 12. Was ... waiting, arrived

Exercise 22   1. has ... been working 2. I'm listening 3. aren't playing 4. hasn't been feeling 5. have ... been doing 6. is ... sitting 7. I've been trying 8. aren't ... getting 9. We've been meaning to 10. have ... been living

Exercise 23   1. why they can't come to the picnic 2. what they're *(= they are)* saying on the loudspeaker 3. what kind of car they bought 4. when they'll *(= they will)* announce the election results 5. how long she's *(= she has)* been studying German 6. where the nearest bus stop is 7. who he married 8. why he wants to quit his job

Exercise 24   A) 1. more ... than, less 2. more ... than, fewer 3. less ... than, more 4. more ... than, fewer

Exercise 24 (cont'd.)   B) 1. as much ... as   2. as many ... as   3. as many ... as   4. as much ... as   5. as many ... as   6. as many ... as

Exercise 25   A) 1. How's *(= How is)* your last name spelled? 2. Your call will be returned this afternoon. 3. Richard wasn't told about the meeting. 4. Where will the new hotel be built? 5. All packages are sent via air mail. 6. Was a 15% tip added to the bill? 7. Jim's apartment was broken into; his stereo was stolen. 8. Red wine isn't *(= is not)* usually drunk with chicken. 9. The bills aren't paid until the first of the month. 10. The repair job wasn't done right.

B) 1. Were your reservations confirmed by the travel agent? 2. The presentation at today's meeting will be given by Mr. Harper. 3. Was Mary's French class taught by Mrs. Hunt last year? 4. Are all the checks made out by the accounting department? 5. A lot of electronic equipment is exported by Japan. 6. The book *Huckleberry Finn* was written by Mark Twain. 7. Mr. Taylor will be operated on by a famous surgeon. 8. The museum is visited by thousands of people every year. 9. The dog was hit by a car while it was crossing the street. 10. People without college degrees aren't hired by Bill's company.

Exercise 26   1. wouldn't he, he would   2. haven't we, we have   3. should I, you shouldn't   4. doesn't she, she does   5. hasn't he, he has   6. am I, you're not   7. isn't she, she is   8. do you, I don't   9. didn't they, they did   10. does it, it doesn't

Exercise 27   1. hasn't been cashed   2. did ... happen   3. was promoted   4. is .. being held   5. Was ... working   6. won't be picked up   7. walks   8. Has ... been found   9. will be called   10. Didn't ... enjoy   11. was taken   12. 've *(= I have)* said   13. are being considered   14. aren't *(= are not)* required   15. were delayed

Exercise 28   1. exciting   2. interested   3. satisfied   4. exhausting   5. confusing   6. boring   7. interesting   8. broken   9. unknown   10. embarrassing   11. challenging   12. bored

Exercise 29 1. open 2. stay up 3. fixed 4. typed 5. done 6. hold 7. painted 8. go over 9. installed 10. leave

Exercise 30 A) 1. herself 2. ourselves 3. themselves 4. myself 5. himself 6. yourself 7. himself 8. itself

B) 1. themselves 2. each other 3. themselves 4. each other 5. each other 6. each other 7. themselves 8. each other

Exercise 31 1. The house should be cleaned before the guests arrive. 2. The typewriter can be repaired this afternoon. 3. All the passports must be stamped. 4. These letters have to be signed as soon as possible. 5. The car shouldn't be left unlocked. 6. This report must be typed before the meeting. 7. Cars shouldn't be parked in front of the driveway. 8. Reservations don't have to be made more than a day in advance. 9. The jacket may be returned if it doesn't fit. 10. The repair job can't be done in less than a day. 11. The filing should be done every morning. 12. Bills may not be paid with a personal check. 13. Mr. Crawford can be reached at home in the evening. 14. The package might not be received until Monday. 15. These batteries will have to be replaced.

Exercise 32 1. try it on 2. call him back 3. look them over 4. pick him up 5. call it off 6. give it up 7. turn it down 8. put them away 9. fill it out 10. makes them up 11. throw them away 12. think it over

Exercise 33 1. When we saw Paula, she'd *(= she had)* just returned from Paris. 2. When John got to the bank, it hadn't closed yet. 3. When Jill went home, she still hadn't finished the report. 4. When Gary's letter came, I'd *(= I had)* already spoken to him. 5. When I went to the garage, they still hadn't fixed my car. 6. When Ted phoned me, I'd *(= I had)* just tried to call him. 7. When the Bells got to the party, dinner hadn't been served yet. 8. When Mrs. Drake asked for the report, we'd *(= we had)* already finished it. 9. When I finished breakfast, Tommy still hadn't left for school. 10. When Mary finished school, she hadn't met her husband yet.

Exercise 34 1. hadn't written 2. did ... learn 3. haven't received 4. was leaving 5. didn't ... make 6. Had ... eaten 7. has been showing 8. had ... been waiting 9. wasn't feeling 10. hadn't ... flown 11. Had ... left 12. did ... stay

Exercise 35 1. b 2. b 3. a 4. b 5. b 6. a 7. a 8. b 9. b 10. a 11. b 12. a

Exercise 36 1. advertise 2. competitions 3. produce 4. satisfactory 5. inheritance 6. scientist 7. entertaining 8. decisions 9. suggestion 10. central

Exercise 37 1. he'd *(= he had)* forgotten his wallet at home 2. Mr. Nelson's office was on the 12th floor 3. he'd *(= he would)* have the T.V. fixed as soon as possible 4. he'd *(= he had)* gone to a concert over the weekend 5. the plane would take off on time 6. they hadn't been notified about the meeting 7. she'd *(= she would)* have a table for us in a few minutes 8. his brother didn't live in Chicago anymore 9. they wouldn't be able to come to the party 10. she/he couldn't get me a reservation for the 21st

Exercise 38 1. 'd *(= had)* better 2. would rather 3. would ... rather 4. had better not 5. 'd *(= would)* rather not 6. 'd *(= had)* better 7. would rather 8. 'd *(= had)* better not 9. 'd *(= had)* better 10. Would ... rather 11. would rather not 12. had better not

Exercise 39 1. Carol asked me how long I would be staying in London. 2. Bob asked John if Janet had come back from lunch yet. 3. Sheila asked the repairman when she could pick up her radio. 4. I asked my husband if he had complained to the manager. 5. Mrs. Hall called to ask how late the store was open. 6. I asked Anne if Joe would have time to read the memo before the meeting. 7. My friend asked if Linda needed any help decorating for the party. 8. Jill askedhow many people had been invited to the wedding reception. 9. Mr. Morgan asked if all the sales figures had been turned in. 10. The operator asked Ken if he had dialed the number correctly. 11. Tom asked me when I had gotten back from Tokyo. 12. Mrs. Adams asked us if

Exercise 39 (cont'd.) we could come to dinner next Saturday. 13. Patty asked Ted why he hadn't gone to the meeting. 14. My wife asked me how long I had been waiting for her. 15. I asked when Mr. Butler had been transferred to Chicago.

Exercise 40 1. delivered 2. call 3. to do 4. quit 5. painted 6. to water 7. fixed 8. to speak 9. change 10. held 11. to put 12. to have 13. to carry 14. left 15. to keep

Exercise 41 A) 1. didn't have to, wouldn't be 2. weren't, wouldn't eat 3. wouldn't play, didn't live 4. weren't tied up, wouldn't have to 5. wouldn't run, didn't have

B) 1. could take, had 2. were, would see 3. would get ... done, could help 4. exercised, would be 5. lived, could walk

Exercise 42 1. I hope not. I hope he doesn't have to work late again tonight. 2. I guess not. I guess he isn't at home. 3. I hope so. I hope she can give us a ride to the train station. 4. I don't think so. I don't think he made a mistake in his calculations. 5. I guess so. I guess she should sign these letters before she leaves. 6. I hope not. I hope we won't have to wait long for a table. 7. I think so. I think they discussed the contract at the meeting. 8. I guess not. I guess the mail hasn't been picked up. 9. I hope not. I hope I don't have to see the dentist again. 10. I don't think so. I don't think we'll have any trouble finding a hotel.

Exercise 43 1. It was hard for Theresa to learn to use the word processor. 2. Was it a good idea for us to pay the bill before it was due? 3. It wasn't necessary for the company to raise its prices. 4. Would it be possible for me to have next Tuesday off? 5. It was better for Mr. Spencer to attend the meeting, too. 6. Why was it so important for Mrs. Tucker to know the details of the contract? 7. It was impossible for Brad to accept the job offer. 8. It will be difficult for the Boston plant to meet its quota. 9. Why is it important for the salesmen to be familiar with the products? 10. It would be better for you to call the personnel office today. 11. It was a good idea

Exercise 43 (cont'd.) for the Blakes to make reservations. 12. It's impossible for us to get hold of Paul during the day.

Exercise 44 1. so 2. such 3. so 4. such 5. such 6. so 7. such 8. so 9. so 10. such 11. so 12. such

Exercise 45 1. see 2. arrived, came in 3. have ... known 4. 've *(= have)* been waiting, hasn't ... taken 5. 'm *(= am)* not watching 6. will check out 7. didn't have to, 's *(= has)* made 8. Do ... go out 9. had, 's *(= is)* ... making 10. Were ... playing 11. won't be finished 12. had been picked up 13. be eaten 14. had ... been 15. won't catch, don't hurry

Exercise 46 1. in 2. until 3. ago 4. during, at 5. for 6. on, at 7. since 8. by 9. for 10. since 11. during 12. in 13. until, now 14. on 15. by, at

Exercise 47 1. gets 2. Would ... take 3. were 4. can ... reach 5. won't leave 6. will check 7. offered 8. isn't 9. arrive 10. wouldn't drive 11. will ... do 12. couldn't afford

Exercise 48 1. Cheryl and Mike are going to Florida on vacation. 2. Their friends said that Florida was a nice place for a vacation. 3. They had a travel agent make reservations at a good hotel. 4. Their plane reservations were made by the travel agent, too. 5. The weather should be great this time of year. 6. They want to spend at least two days at Disneyworld. 7. The travel agent told them they couldn't see everything in one day. 8. They've been looking forward to the trip for months. 9. They've already packed their bags. 10. It sounds like a great vacation, doesn't it?

TAPESCRIPT

Tape 1   DO YOU TWO KNOW EACH OTHER?

John Morgan and his wife, Susan, are at a concert this evening. During the intermission, they go to the lobby for a soft drink.

Susan: Aren't you glad we came to the concert, John? The orchestra is terrific.

John: Well, at least I didn't fall asleep. No, really, you're absolutely right — we don't go out often enough. Hey ...!!

Lucy: Oh! I'm sorry! I didn't see you. It's orange juice ... and it's all over your jacket!

John: No problem. This jacket's been through so much already, I don't even worry about it anymore. There ... you see, it's gone now.

Lucy: Are you sure? I'm really sorry. I feel terrible.

John: It's O.K., really. No harm done. By the way, I'm John, and this is my wife, Susan.

Lucy: Nice to meet you, John, Susan. I'm Lucy.

Susan: Are you enjoying the concert, Lucy?

Lucy: Oh, yes! In fact, it's my first night out in New York. My husband, Dave, and I recently moved here from a small town in Ohio. To tell you the truth, we're still trying to get used to life in a big city.

Susan: Don't worry. You're going to love New York. Everyone does.

Lucy: I hope so. Dave's working in a big company for the first time, and he says the pressure is awful. He works late almost every night. In fact, he's calling a client right now. Can you believe it? A business call in the middle of a concert! He has a very demanding boss, and Dave is trying his best to make a good impression. It's the first time we've gone out in months!

Susan: Hmm ... that sounds familiar. I'm always trying to get John away from *his* work, too!

Lucy: Oh, here comes Dave now. Dave! Over here! Susan, John, I'd like you to meet ...

Dave: Mr. Morgan! What ... what are you doing here?

Lucy: Do you two know each other?

Dave: Sure, honey. This is my boss at Superior Products, John Morgan.

Lucy: Oh! Well ... I ... I guess it's not such a big city after all!

Now, let's listen to the conversation once again ... and then answer some questions.

Susan: Aren't you glad we came to the concert, John? The orchestra is terrific.

John: Well, at least I didn't fall asleep. No, really, you're absolutely right — we don't go out often enough. Hey ...!!

Lucy: Oh! I'm sorry! I didn't see you. It's orange juice ... and it's all over your jacket!

John: No problem. This jacket's been through so much already, I don't even worry about it anymore. There ... you see, it's gone now.

Answer!

Is Mrs. Morgan sorry she and John went to the concert?	No, she's not sorry they went to the concert.
She's glad they went, isn't she?	Yes, she's glad they went.
Did someone spill orange juice on John's jacket?	Yes, someone spilled orange juice on his jacket.
But John's not worried about it, is he?	No, he's not worried about it.
It's been through so much already, he doesn't worry about it anymore, right?	That's right, it's been through so much already, he doesn't worry about it anymore.

Very good!

Now *you* ask the questions.

Repeat!
The Morgans are standing in the lobby.
Where are they standing?

John's wearing a jacket. Question? What is ...	What is he wearing?
He isn't speaking to Janet Brown. Question? Who is ...	Who is he speaking to?
It isn't a rock-and-roll concert. Question? What kind of ...	What kind of concert is it?

Good! Very good!

Now let's listen again.

John: This jacket's been through so much already, I don't even worry about it anymore. There ... you see, it's gone now.

Lucy: Are you sure? I'm really sorry. I feel terrible.

John: It's O.K., really. No harm done. By the way, I'm John, and this is my wife, Susan.

Lucy: Nice to meet you, John, Susan. I'm Lucy.

Susan: Are you enjoying the concert, Lucy?

Lucy: Oh, yes! In fact, it's my first night out in New York. My husband, Dave, and I recently moved here from a small town in Ohio.

Answer!

Did Lucy spill orange juice on John's jacket?	Yes, she spilled orange juice on his jacket.
Did she feel terrible about it?	Yes, she felt terrible about it.
But John said there was no harm done, didn't he?	Yes, he said there was no harm done.
Are Lucy and her husband, Dave, from New York?	No, they're not from New York.
They recently moved to New York from a small town in Ohio, right?	That's right, they recently moved to New York from a small town in Ohio.

Very good! Excellent!

Listen again!

Lucy: My husband, Dave, and I recently moved here from a small town in Ohio. To tell you the truth, we're still trying to get used to life in a big city.

Susan: Don't worry. You're going to love New York. Everyone does.

Lucy: I hope so. Dave's working in a big company for the first time, and he says the pressure is awful. He works late almost every night. In fact, he's calling a client right now. Can you believe it? A business call in the middle of a concert! He has a very demanding boss, and Dave is trying his best to make a good impression.

Answer!

Lucy and her husband, Dave, come from a small town, don't they?	Yes, they come from a small town.
Are they used to life in a big city?	No, they're not used to life in a big city.
They're still trying to get used to life in a big city, aren't they?	Yes, they're still trying to get used to life in a big city.

Does Dave work late a lot?
He works late almost every night, right?
What's Dave doing right now? Is he relaxing or is he calling a client?
He's making a business call in the middle of the concert, right?

Yes, he works late a lot.
That's right, he works late almost every night.

He's calling a client.
That's right, he's making a business call in the middle of the concert.

Very good!

Repeat!
Dave is making a business call.
He often makes business calls.

He's speaking to a client.
Answer! He often speaks ...

He often speaks to clients.

He's working late.
He often ...

He often works late.

He's talking about business.
He ...

He often talks about business.

He's calling in the evening.
He ...

He often calls in the evening.

Very good! That was excellent!

Let's listen again. Lucy is still talking to the Morgans.

   Lucy: It's the first time we've gone out in months!

  Susan: Hmm ... that sounds familiar. I'm always trying to get John away from *his* work, too!

   Lucy: Oh, here comes Dave now. Dave! Over here! Susan, John, I'd like you to meet ...

  Dave: Mr. Morgan! What ... what are you doing here?

   Lucy: Do you two know each other?

  Dave: Sure, honey. This is my boss at Superior Products, John Morgan.

   Lucy: Oh! Well ... I ...`I guess it's not such a big city after all!

Answer!
Lucy and Dave don't go out very often, do they?

No, they don't go out very often.

Did that surprise Susan, or did it sound familiar?	It sounded familiar.
Why? Is Susan always trying to get John away from his work, too?	Yes, she's always trying to get him away from his work, too.
Did Lucy introduce her husband, Dave?	Yes, she introduced him.
But Dave and Mr. Morgan already know each other, don't they?	Yes, they already know each other.
They already know each other because Mr. Morgan is Dave's boss, right?	That's right, they already know each other because Mr. Morgan is Dave's boss.

Excellent!

Now, listen to the conversation once again. This time, listen ... and repeat!

Aren't you glad we came to the concert, John?
The orchestra is terrific.

Well, at least I didn't fall asleep.
No, really, you're absolutely right
we don't go out often enough.
Hey!

Oh, I'm sorry! I didn't see you.
It's orange juice ... and it's all over your jacket!
I'm really sorry. I feel terrible.

It's O.K., really. No harm done.
By the way, I'm John, and this is my wife, Susan.

Nice to meet you, John, Susan. I'm Lucy.
Oh, here comes Dave now.
Susan, John, I'd like you to meet ...

Mr. Morgan! What ... what are you doing here?

Do you two know each other?

Sure, honey. This is my boss at Superior Products, John Morgan.

Well, the intermission is over, and the concert is about to continue. But this tape, Tape 1, is about to end.

This is the end of Tape 1.

Tape 2   WHEN CAN WE GET TOGETHER?

Jim Reynolds works in the Marketing Department at Superior Products. He wants to get in touch with John Morgan to talk over some ideas he has for a new advertising campaign. He called Morgan's office first thing in the morning, hoping to catch him before he got tied up.

Janet: Mr. Morgan's office. May I help you?

Jim: Janet, this is Jim Reynolds. I'd like to talk to John if he's free.

Janet: Oh, hello, Mr. Reynolds. I'm sorry, he was in earlier, but he had to leave for a meeting. He should be back around 11 o'clock.

Jim: Just my luck! I really wanted to get hold of him to set up a meeting for today or tomorrow. When he gets back, could you ask him to return my call?

Janet: Sure. I'll give him the message as soon as he gets in.

When Mr. Morgan returned, Janet gave him the message and he returned Jim's call right away.

Secretary: Good morning, Jim Reynold's office.

John: This is John Morgan returning his call. Is he in?

Secretary: Yes, he is, Mr. Morgan. He's expecting your call. He's on the other line right now. Would you like to hold or can he call you back?

John: I'll hold. ...

Jim: Hi, John. Sorry to keep you waiting. Listen, I'd like to get together and discuss some ideas for the new ad campaign. Could we possibly meet tomorrow morning?

John: Sorry, Jim, I've got a 9 o'clock appointment and I may be tied up all morning. How about lunch? We can grab a quick sandwich at that little place around the corner. About 12:30?

Jim: Great. See you then.

Now let's listen to the conversation once again. And then ... answer some questions.

Janet: Mr. Morgan's office. May I help you?

Jim: Janet, this is Jim Reynolds. I'd like to talk to John if he's free.

Janet: Oh, hello, Mr. Reynolds. I'm sorry, he was in earlier, but he had to leave for a meeting. He should be back around 11 o'clock.

Answer!
Did Mr. Morgan answer the phone?

No, he didn't answer the phone.

Who answered the phone, Janet?

Yes, Janet answered the phone.

But Jim Reynolds didn't call to talk to Janet, did he?

No, he didn't call to talk to Janet.

Who did he call to talk to, Janet or Mr. Morgan?

He called to talk to Mr. Morgan.

Was Mr. Morgan free, or did he have to leave for a meeting?

He had to leave for a meeting.

What time should he be back, around 11?

Yes, he should be back around 11.

He had to leave for a meeting, but he should be back around 11, right?

That's right, he had to leave for a meeting, but he should be back around 11.

Very good!

Repeat!
Mr. Morgan will probably be back at 11.
He should be back at 11.

He'll probably be on time.
Answer! He should be ...

He should be on time.

He'll probably be free for lunch.
He should ...

He should be free for lunch.

His meeting will probably be over soon.
It should ...

It should be over soon.

It probably won't last too long.
It ...

It shouldn't last too long.

Good! Very good!

Listen again! Jim Reynolds and Janet are still on the phone.

    Janet: I'm sorry, Mr. Morgan was in earlier, but he had to leave for a meeting. He should be back around 11 o'clock.

    Jim: Just my luck! I really wanted to get hold of him to set up a meeting for today or tomorrow. When he gets back, could you ask him to return my call?

    Janet: Sure. I'll give him the message as soon as he gets in.

Answer!

Would Jim like to set up a meeting?	Yes, he'd like to set up a meeting.
That's why he wants to get hold of Mr. Morgan, isn't it?	Yes, that's why he wants to get hold of Mr. Morgan.
Does Jim want Mr. Morgan to return his call?	Yes, he wants him to return his call.
He wants him to return his call when he gets back, right?	That's right, he wants him to return his call when he gets back.
Did Janet say she would give him Jim's message?	Yes, she said she would give him Jim's message.
She'll give him the message as soon as he gets in, right?	That's right, she'll give him the message as soon as he gets in.

Very good! Excellent!

Now *you* ask the questions.

Repeat!
Mr. Reynolds doesn't want to have a meeting in a week.
When does he want to have a meeting?

He doesn't have to meet with Janet.
Question? Who does he ...   Who does he have to meet with?

He doesn't want to have the meeting at his home.
Where does ...   Where does he want to have the meeting?

He doesn't want to talk about sports.
What ...   What does he want to talk about?

There won't be ten people at the meeting.
How many ...   How many people will there be at the meeting?

Very good!

Let's listen again. Mr. Morgan is returning Jim Reynold's call.

   Secretary: Good morning, Jim Reynold's office.

   John: This is John Morgan returning his call. Is he in?

   Secretary: Yes, he is, Mr. Morgan. He's expecting your call. He's on the other line right now. Would you like to hold or can he call you back?

   John: I'll hold. ...

Jim: Hi, John. Sorry to keep you waiting.

Answer!

Did Mr. Morgan return Jim Reynold's call?	Yes, he returned his call.
Who answered the phone, Mr. Reynolds or his secretary?	His secretary answered the phone.
Mr. Morgan couldn't speak to Jim right away, could he?	No, he couldn't speak to him right away.
Why not? Was Jim speaking on the other line?	Yes, he was speaking on the other line.
He was speaking on the other line, so Mr. Morgan had to hold, right?	That's right, he was speaking on the other line, so Mr. Morgan had to hold.

Good!

Now, let's listen to the rest of the conversation.

Jim: Hi, John. Listen, I'd like to get together and discuss some ideas for the new ad campaign. Could we possibly meet tomorrow morning?

John: Sorry, Jim, I've got a 9 o'clock appointment and I may be tied up all morning. How about lunch? We can grab a quick sandwich at that little place around the corner. About 12:30?

Jim: Great. See you then.

Answer!

Does Jim want to get together with Mr. Morgan?	Yes, he wants to get together with him.
What does he want to discuss, his salary or the new ad campaign?	He wants to discuss the new ad campaign.
He'd like to get together and discuss some ideas for the new ad campaign, right?	That's right, he'd like to get together and discuss some ideas for the new ad campaign.
Is Mr. Morgan free tomorrow morning?	No, he isn't free tomorrow morning.
He has a 9 o'clock appointment and he may be tied up all morning, right?	That's right, he has a 9 o'clock appointment and he may be tied up all morning.
Is that why he and Jim are going to meet for lunch instead?	Yes, that's why they're going to meet for lunch instead.

They're going to grab a quick sandwich at a little place around the corner, aren't they?	Yes, they're going to grab a quick sandwich at a little place around the corner.

Very good!

Now, let's listen to the conversation once again. This time, listen ... and repeat!

Mr. Morgan's office. May I help you?

Janet, this is Jim Reynolds.
I'd like to talk to John if he's free.

I'm sorry, he was in earlier, but he had to leave for a meeting.

Just my luck!
When he gets back, could you ask him to return my call?

Sure. I'll give him the message as soon as he gets in.

Good morning. Jim Reynold's office.

This is John Morgan returning his call. Is he in?

Yes, he is, Mr. Morgan. He's expecting your call.
He's on the other line right now.
Would you like to hold or can he call you back?

I'll hold.

Hi, John. Sorry to keep you waiting.
Listen, I'd like to get together and discuss some ideas for the new ad campaign.

Sorry, Jim, I've got a nine o'clock appointment and I may be tied up all morning. How about lunch?

We can grab a quick sandwich at that little place around the corner.

Great. See you then.

Well, it looks like Mr. Morgan and Jim Reynolds are going to meet for lunch. Their conversation is over now, and this tape, Tape 2, is over, too.

This is the end of Tape 2.

Tape 3   BACK ALREADY?

Janet is in the company cafeteria. She's just paid for her food and is looking for a place to sit when she notices her friend Bob Elliott sitting alone at a table in the corner.

Janet: Hey, Bob! I thought you were on vacation.

Bob: I was, but I came back last night. I was only away for three days. They had an emergency in the office, and my boss called and asked if I could cut my vacation short. It's too bad I left my number with his secretary.

Janet: Where did you go?

Bob: To Washington. I have friends there, and they invited me to come down and spend some time with them.

Janet: Washington? Really? I went to college there. What did you see? Did you visit the White House?

Bob: We sure did. Then we drove around and visited all the famous tourist sights. I think it's a great city!

Janet: I do, too. Did you get to see the Picasso exhibit at the National Gallery? There was a big article about it in the *New York Times* last Sunday.

Bob: We tried, but it was too crowded. The line stretched halfway around the block. We visited the Air and Space Museum instead. What a place! We were there almost four hours, and we didn't even see half of it. Then, that night, my friends fixed me up with a date and we went out to a disco. We didn't get back till three in the morning.

Janet: It sounds like you had quite a time!

Bob: I did. But I learned one lesson ... when you take your vacation, don't tell your boss where you're going!

Now, let's listen to the conversation again. And then ... answer some questions.

Janet: Hey, Bob! I thought you were on vacation.

Bob: I was, but I came back last night. I was only away for three days. They had an emergency in the office, and my boss called and asked if I could cut my vacation short. It's too bad I left my number with his secretary.

Answer!

Was Bob out of town on business?	No, he wasn't out of town on business.
He was on vacation, wasn't he?	Yes, he was on vacation.
Did Bob come back early because he got sick?	No, he didn't come back early because he got sick.
He came back early because they had an emergency in the office, didn't he?	Yes, he came back early because they had an emergency in the office.

He was on vacation, but he came back early because they had an emergency in the office, right?

That's right, he was on vacation, but he came back early because they had an emergency in the office.

Very good!

Now, *you* ask the questions.

Repeat!
Janet didn't go to Washington.
Who went to Washington?

Janet didn't stay with friends there.
Question? Who ...

Who stayed with friends there?

Janet didn't think Bob was away on business.
Who ...

Who thought he was away on business?

Janet didn't get a call from the boss.
Who ...

Who got a call from the boss?

Janet didn't come back early.
Who ...

Who came back early?

Janet didn't have a short vacation.
Who ...

Who had a short vacation?

Good! Very good!

Janet and Bob are still talking about Bob's vacation. Listen!

   Janet: Where did you go?

   Bob: To Washington. I have friends there, and they invited me to come down and spend some time with them.

   Janet: Washington? Really? I went to college there. What did you see? Did you visit the White House?

   Bob: We sure did. Then we drove around and visited all the famous tourist sights. I think it's a great city!

Answer!
Where did Bob go on vacation, to Washington or Philadelphia?

He went to Washington.

He has friends there, doesn't he?

Yes, he has friends there.

Did they invite him to come and spend some time with them?

Yes, they invited him to come and spend some time with them.

So, he has friends in Washington and they invited him to come and spend some time with them, right?

That's right, he has friends in Washington and they invited him to come and spend some time with them.

Did Bob and his friends drive around the city and visit all the famous tourist sights?

Yes, they drove around the city and visited all the famous tourist sights.

They didn't forget to see the White House, did they?

No, they didn't forget to see the White House.

Very good! Excellent!

Now, repeat!
Bob takes a vacation every year.
He took a vacation last year, too.

He doesn't stay away long.
He didn't stay away long last year, either.

He visits friends on his vacation.
Answer! He visited friends ...

He visited friends on his vacation last year, too.

He doesn't stay at expensive hotels.
He didn't ...

He didn't stay at expensive hotels last year, either.

He sees all the famous tourist sights.
He ...

He saw all the famous tourist sights last year, too.

He doesn't go sightseeing alone.
He ...

He didn't go sightseeing alone last year, either.

Very good!

Listen again. Bob's still telling Janet about his visit to Washington.

    Bob: I think it's a great city!

    Janet: I do, too. Did you get to see the Picasso exhibit at the National Gallery? There was a big article about it in the *New York Times* last Sunday.

    Bob: We tried, but it was too crowded. The line stretched halfway around the block. We visited the Air and Space Museum instead.

Answer!
Did Bob and his friends get to see the Picasso exhibit?

No, they didn't get to see the Picasso exhibit.

Why? Was it too crowded?

Yes, it was too crowded.

They didn't get to see the Picasso exhibit because it was too crowded, right?	That's right, they didn't get to see the Picasso exhibit because it was too crowded.
Did they visit the Air and Space Museum instead?	Yes, they visited the Air and Space Museum instead.

Excellent!

Now let's listen to the rest of the conversation.

> *Bob:* We visited the Air and Space Museum instead. What a place! We were there almost four hours, and we didn't even see half of it. Then, that night, my friends fixed me up with a date and we went out to a disco. We didn't get back till three in the morning.
>
> *Janet:* It sounds like you had quite a time!
>
> *Bob:* I did. But I learned one lesson ... when you take your vacation, don't tell your boss where you're going!

Answer!

Bob and his friends didn't stay at the Air and Space Museum all day, did they?	No, they didn't stay there all day.
How long did they stay, all day or almost four hours?	They stayed almost four hours.
Did they see everything?	No, they didn't see everything.
They were there almost four hours, and they didn't even see half of it, right?	That's right, they were there almost four hours, and they didn't even see half of it.
That night, Bob's friends fixed him up with a date, didn't they?	Yes, that night they fixed him up with a date.
Where did they go, to a movie or a disco?	They went to a disco.
They went to a disco, and they didn't get back till three in the morning, right?	That's right, they went to a disco, and they didn't get back till three in the morning.

Good! Very good!

Now listen to part of the dialog again. This time, listen ... and repeat!

Hey, Bob! I thought you were on vacation.

I was, but I came back last night.
They had an emergency in the office,
and my boss called and asked if I could cut my vacation short.

Where did you go?

To Washington. I have friends there.

Washington? Really? I went to college there.
I think it's a great city!

I do, too. Did you get to see the Picasso exhibit at the National Gallery?

We tried, but it was too crowded.
We visited the Air and Space Museum instead.
Then, that night, my friends fixed me up with a date
and we went out to a disco.

It sounds like you had quite a time!

I did. But I learned one lesson ...
when you take your vacation, don't tell your boss where you're going!

Well, Bob's vacation in Washington is over, and our time on this tape, Tape 3, is over, too.

This is the end of Tape 3.

Tape 4   I'D LIKE TO SPEAK TO THE MANAGER

Janet is in Los Angeles visiting her sister. She has just arrived at the airport and is standing at the car rental counter.

Janet:	Hello, I'm Janet Brown. I have a reservation for a compact car.
Agent:	Fine. Let's see ... when did you make the reservation?
Janet:	It was last Wednesday, I think.
Agent:	O.K., let me check. Hmm, are you sure you made the reservation with this agency? The computer isn't showing anything in your name.
Janet:	Yes, I'm positive. I called your toll-free number.
Agent:	We've had some trouble with the computer lately ... but it doesn't matter. We still have quite a few cars available.
Janet:	They promised a compact car would be waiting for me when I got here.
Agent:	A compact? I'm sorry, but all our compacts are out. The only thing we have left is a full-size sedan. It's only nineteen dollars a day more than the compact.

Janet: But, that's ridiculous! I don't need a full-size car, and I'm certainly not going to pay more for one. I reserved a compact, and that's what I want!

Agent: But I've already explained, we don't have any compacts available. There's really nothing I can do. You know, our full-size cars are really very nice. They're more comfortable and much more luxurious. And if you think about it, bigger cars are safer.

Janet: Look, why don't you just let me speak to the manager?

Agent: All right, I'll see if he's free ... I'm sorry, Mr. Stephens is tied up right now. But because of the mix-up, he's agreed to let you have a full-size car for the same price as a compact.

Janet: Well ... I appreciate that. Hmm ... it looks like I'll be driving around in style. Oh, by the way, you don't have a red car by any chance, do you? That's my favorite color ...

Now, let's listen to the conversation once again. And then ... answer some questions.

Janet: Hello, I'm Janet Brown. I have a reservation for a compact car.

Agent: Fine. Let's see ... when did you make the reservation?

Janet: It was last Wednesday, I think.

Agent: O.K., let me check. Hmm, are you sure you made the reservation with this agency? The computer isn't showing anything in your name.

Janet: Yes, I'm positive. I called your toll-free number.

Answer!

Did Janet reserve a full-size car?	No, she didn't reserve a full-size car.
She reserved a compact car, didn't she?	Yes, she reserved a compact car.
Did she call the toll-free number when she made the reservation?	Yes, she called the toll-free number when she made the reservation.
But the computer isn't showing anything in her name, is it?	No, the computer isn't showing anything in her name.
She made the reservation, but the computer isn't showing anything in her name, right?	That's right, she made the reservation, but the computer isn't showing anything in her name.

Good!

Repeat!
Janet is going to rent a car.
But she hasn't rented a car yet.

She's going to fill out the forms.
Answer! But she hasn't ...

But she hasn't filled out the forms yet.

She's going to leave the airport.
But she hasn't ...

But she hasn't left the airport yet.

She's going to visit her sister.
But she ...

But she hasn't visited her sister yet.

She's going to see the city.
But ...

But she hasn't seen the city yet.

Good!

Let's listen again.

   Agent: We've had some trouble with the computer lately ... but it doesn't matter. We still have quite a few cars available.

   Janet: They promised a compact car would be waiting for me when I got here.

   Agent: A compact? I'm sorry, but all our compacts are out. The only thing we have left is a full-size sedan. It's only nineteen dollars a day more than the compact.

Answer!
Was Janet promised a compact car?

Yes, she was promised a compact car.

But they don't have any compacts available, do they?

No, they don't have any compacts available.

Are all the compacts out?

Yes, they're all out.

Janet was promised a compact car, but all the compacts are out, right?

That's right, she was promised a compact car, but all the compacts are out.

Very good!

Now, listen again.

   Agent: The only thing we have left is a full-size sedan. It's only nineteen dollars a day more than the compact.

   Janet: But, that's ridiculous! I don't need a full-size car, and I'm certainly not going to pay more for one. I reserved a compact, and that's what I want!

> Agent: But I've already explained, we don't have any compacts available. There's really nothing I can do. You know, our full-size cars are really very nice. They're more comfortable and much more luxurious. And if you think about it, bigger cars are safer.
>
> Janet: Look, why don't you just let me speak to the manager?

Answer!

Do they have a full-size sedan available?	Yes, they have a full-size sedan available.
But Janet didn't reserve a full-size sedan, did she?	No, she didn't reserve a full-size sedan.
She reserved a compact, and that's what she wants, isn't it?	Yes, she reserved a compact, and that's what she wants.
What did the agent say? Did he say there's nothing he can do about the problem?	Yes, he said there's nothing he can do about the problem.
Who does Janet want to speak to, another agent or the manager?	She wants to speak to the manager.
She wants to speak to the manager because the agent said there's nothing he can do, right?	That's right, she wants to speak to the manager because the agent said there's nothing he can do.

Very good!

Repeat!

Janet isn't speaking to the agent now. She's already spoken to the agent.

She isn't explaining the problem now. *Answer!* She's already explained ...	She's already explained the problem.
She isn't making the reservation now. She's already ...	She's already made the reservation.
She isn't arriving at the airport now. She's ...	She's already arrived at the airport.
She isn't getting off the plane now. She's ...	She's already gotten off the plane.

Excellent!

Now, let's listen to the rest of the conversation.

> Janet: Look, why don't you just let me speak to the manager?

Agent:	All right, I'll see if he's free ... I'm sorry, Mr. Stephens is tied up right now. But because of the mix-up, he's agreed to let you have a full-size car for the same price as a compact.
Janet:	Well ... I appreciate that. Hmm ... it looks like I'll be driving around in style. Oh, by the way, you don't have a red car by any chance, do you? That's my favorite color ...

Answer!

Did Janet speak to the manager?	No, she didn't speak to him.
The manager is tied up right now, isn't he?	Yes, he's tied up right now.
Is Janet going to get a small car?	No, she isn't going to get a smal car.
She's going to get a full-size car for the same price as a compact, right?	That's right, she's going to get a full-size car for the same price as a compact.
She'll be driving around in style after all, right?	That's right, she'll be driving around in style after all.

Very good!

Now, listen to the conversation once again. This time, listen ... and repeat!

Hello, I'm Janet Brown.
I have a reservation for a compact car.
Fine. Let's see ... when did you make the reservation?
It was last Wednesday, I think.
Are you sure you made the reservation with this agency?
Yes, I'm positive. I called your toll-free number.
We've had some trouble with the computer lately, but it doesn't matter.
We still have quite a few cars available.
They promised a compact car would be waiting for me when I got here.
I'm sorry, but all our compacts are out.
The only thing we have left is a full-size sedan.
I don't need a full-size car, and I'm certainly not going to pay more for one.
Look, why don't you just let me speak to the manager?
I'm sorry, Mr. Stephens is tied up right now.
But, because of the mix-up, he's agreed to let you have a full-size car for the same price as a compact.

Well ... I appreciate that.
Oh, by the way, you don't have a red car by any chance, do you? That's my favorite color ...

Well, it looks like Janet's conversation at the car rental agency is about to end ... and our conversation is about to end, too.

This is the end of Tape 4.

Tape 5   WHAT'S GOING ON OUT THERE?

Kevin Williams, manager of Superior Products' London office, is in New York on business for a few days. Right now, he and his wife, Sarah, are in their hotel room.

Kevin: This is a much better hotel than the one we stayed at last time, don't you think, Sarah?

Sarah: Oh, yes, it's very nice. Goodness, what a trip! We've been up since five this morning. And I didn't get a wink of sleep on the plane. I think I'll take a short nap.

Kevin: That sounds like a good idea. A little sleep and we'll be as good as new. Can you believe it's only 10:30 in the morning here? I certainly don't feel like doing much today. I think the jetlag is getting to me already.

Sarah: Kevin, do you hear that dreadful pounding noise? What *ever* are they doing out there?

Kevin: Hmm ... it sounds as if they're tearing up the street.

Sarah: Just what we needed! We'll never get any sleep if that keeps up. Do you think we should see if they can give us a different room?

Kevin: Good idea. I'll call the front desk.

Clerk: Front desk. May I help you?

Kevin: This is Kevin Williams in Room 217. There's a lot of pounding going on outside our window. My wife and I are quite tired, and we're not going to be able to get much rest with all that commotion going on. Could you possibly give us another room?

Clerk: Oh, I'm sorry, Mr. Williams. They're doing some construction across the street. I'm sure we can arrange something. Let's see ... yes, I can give you a very nice room on the 7th floor overlooking Central Park. It's very quiet, and the view is lovely.

Kevin: Splendid. There'll be no change in the rate, I hope.

Clerk: No, sir. Not under the circumstances. I'll send the bellman right up. He'll show you to the room and take care of your luggage. And, once again, I apologize for the inconvenience.

Kevin: That's quite all right. Thank you. ... Well, Sarah, they're going to move us to another room. The gentleman said it has a lovely view of Central Park. Sarah? ... Sarah? ... Oh, dear, she's fallen asleep!

Now, let's listen to the conversation once again. And then ... answer some questions.

Kevin: This is a much better hotel than the one we stayed at last time, don't you think, Sarah?

Sarah: Oh, yes, it's very nice. Goodness, what a trip! We've been up since five this morning. And I didn't get a wink of sleep on the plane. I think I'll take a short nap.

Kevin: That's sounds like a good idea. A little sleep and we'll be as good as new. Can you believe it's only 10:30 in the morning here? I certainly don't feel like doing much today. I think the jetlag is getting to me already.

Answer!
Did Sarah sleep well on the plane?

No, she didn't sleep well on the plane.

What does Sarah want to do? Does she want to take a long walk or a short nap?

She wants to take a short nap.

And what about Kevin? Does he feel like doing much today?

No, he doesn't feel like doing much today either.

What's wrong? Is the jetlag getting to him already?

Yes, the jetlag is getting to him already.

Are Kevin and Sarah staying at a nice hotel?

Yes, they're staying at a nice hotel.

It's a much better hotel than the one they stayed at last time, right?

That's right, it's a much better hotel than the one they stayed at last time.

Very good!

Now, *you* ask the questions.

Repeat!
They stayed at a hotel last time.
Will they stay at a hotel next time, too?

They visited friends last time.
Question? Will they visit ...

Will they visit friends next time, too?

Kevin came to New York on business last time.
Question? Will he come ...

Will he come to New York on business next time, too?

Sarah made the trip with him last time.
Question? Will she ...

Will she make the trip with him next time, too?

They did a lot of shopping last time.
Question? Will ...

Will they do a lot of shopping next time, too?

Very good! Excellent!

Now, let's listen again.

   Sarah: Kevin, do you hear that dreadful pounding noise? What *ever* are they doing out there?

   Kevin: Hmm ... it sounds as if they're tearing up the street.

   Sarah: Just what we needed! We'll never get any sleep if that keeps up. Do you think we should see if they can give us a different room?

   Kevin: Good idea. I'll call the front desk.

Answer!
Were Kevin and Sarah able to get to sleep?

No, they weren't able to get to sleep.

Why? Did they hear some kind of noise outside their window?

Yes, they heard some kind of noise outside their window.

Who's Kevin going to call, the front desk or another hotel?

He's going to call the front desk.

He's going to call the front desk to ask for a different room, right?

That's right, he's going to call the front desk to ask for a different room.

Very good!

Repeat!
He's going to ask for a different room.
He'll ask for a different room when he calls the front desk.

He's going to give his name.
He'll give his name when he calls the front desk.

He's going to speak to the manager.
Answer! He'll speak to the manager when ...

He'll speak to the manager when he calls the front desk.

He's going to explain the problem.
He'll explain the problem ...

He'll explain the problem when he calls the front desk.

He's going to ask for a quieter room.
He'll ask for ...

He'll ask for a quieter room when he calls the front desk.

He's going to get the problem solved.
He'll ...

He'll get the problem solved when he calls the front desk.

Very good! Excellent!

Now, let's listen again. Kevin is calling the front desk.

Clerk: Front desk. May I help you?

Kevin: This is Kevin Williams in Room 217. There's a lot of pounding going on outside our window. My wife and I are quite tired, and we're not going to be able to get much rest with all that commotion going on. Could you possibly give us another room?

Clerk: Oh, I'm sorry, Mr. Williams. They're doing some construction across the street. I'm sure we can arrange something. Let's see ... yes, I can give you a very nice room on the seventh floor overlooking Central Park. It's very quiet, and the view is lovely.

Kevin: Splendid.

Answer!

Are Kevin and Sarah happy with their room?

No, they're not happy with it.

What's wrong? Is there a lot of pounding going on outside their window?

Yes, there's a lot of pounding going on outside their window.

Did the clerk know about the commotion?

Yes, he knew about it.

I beg your pardon? What did the clerk know about?

He knew about the commotion.

Does he have another room available?

Yes, he has another room available.

Good! Very good!

Now listen again.

Kevin: There'll be no change in the rate, I hope.

Clerk: No, sir. Not under the circumstances. I'll send the bellman right up. He'll show you to the room and take care of your luggage. And, once again, I apologize for the inconvenience.

Kevin: That's quite all right. Thank you. ... Well, Sarah, they're going to move us to another room. The gentleman said it has a lovely view of Central Park. Sarah? ... Sarah? ... Oh, dear, she's fallen asleep!

Answer!

Are Kevin and Sarah going to move to another room?	Yes, they're going to move to another room.
There won't be any change in the rate, will there?	No, there won't be any change in the rate.
Did the desk clerk apologize for the inconvenience?	Yes, he apologized for the inconvenience.
I beg your pardon? What did he apologize for?	He apologized for the inconvenience.

Very good!

Now, listen to the conversation once again. This time, listen ... and repeat!

Goodness, what a trip!
We've been up since five this morning.
I think I'll take a short nap.
Do you hear that dreadful pounding noise?
We'll never get any sleep if that keeps up.

I'll call the front desk. ...
This is Kevin Williams in Room 217.
My wife and I are quite tired
and we're not going to be able to get much rest with all that commotion going on.
Could you possibly give us another room?

Yes, I can give you a very nice room on the seventh floor overlooking Central Park.

There'll be no change in the rate, I hope.

No, sir. Not under the circumstances.
I'll send the bellman right up.
And, once again, I apologize for the inconvenience.

That's quite all right. Thank you.

Well, Kevin's conversation with the desk clerk is over. And this tape, Tape 5, is over, too.

This is the end of Tape 5.

Tape 6 — I'LL TAKE IT!

Mr. Morgan was reading the newspaper one day and saw that *Macy's* was having a big sale on men's clothes. He went to the store at lunch time, and a salesman came up to him.

Salesman: May I help you with something?

Mr. Morgan: Yes. I see you're having a sale on sports jackets.

Salesman: That's right. All our jackets are on sale for the next three days. Were you looking for anything in particular?

Mr. Morgan: Well, a few minutes ago you were showing a gentleman a dark blue winter jacket. I was thinking of something along those lines.

Salesman: That's a very popular jacket. We've been selling quite a few of them lately. What size do you wear?

Mr. Morgan: I take a 40 regular.

Salesman: All the 40's are on this rack over here. This is the one the gentleman was trying on. It's 100% English wool.

Mr. Morgan: I like the style. It's not a bad color, either. I also like this gray one here. I'd like to try both on, if I can.

Salesman: Certainly. The mirror is over there in the corner, by the window. ... Well, how does it feel?

Mr. Morgan: It feels a little small. Maybe I should try it in a larger size.

Salesman: I'm sorry. We don't have that color in size 42. But we do have the gray one in that size. Would you like to try it on?

Mr. Morgan: All right. Ah ... this one fits much better. Yes, it's perfect. I think I'll take it!

Salesman: Will that be cash or charge?

Mr. Morgan: Charge, please.

Salesman: Fine. Oh, by the way, if you'd like to look at some shirts to go with that, there's a very good sale going on in the shirt department.

Mr. Morgan: Thanks. I'll have a look.

Now, let's listen to the conversation once again. And then ... answer some questions.

Salesman: May I help you with something?

Mr. Morgan: Yes. I see you're having a sale on sports jackets.

Salesman:	That's right. All our jackets are on sale for the next three days. Were you looking for anything in particular?
Mr. Morgan:	Well, a few minutes ago you were showing a gentleman a dark blue winter jacket. I was thinking of something along those lines.
Salesman:	That's a very popular jacket. We've been selling quite a few of them lately.

Answer!

Are they having a sale on shoes or jackets?	They're having a sale on jackets.
They're having a sale on sports jackets, aren't they?	Yes, they're having a sale on sports jackets.
How long are they going to be on sale, for the next three weeks or the next three days?	They're going to be on sale for the next three days.
Was the salesman just showing someone a jacket a few minutes ago?	Yes, he was just showing someone a jacket a few minutes ago.
Was he showing him a summer jacket?	No, he wasn't showing him a summer jacket.
He was showing him a dark blue winter jacket, wasn't he?	Yes, he was showing him a dark blue winter jacket.
Mr. Morgan was thinking of something along those lines, wasn't he?	Yes, he was thinking of something along those lines.
Aha! The salesman was showing someone a dark blue jacket, and Mr. Morgan was thinking of something along those lines, right?	That's right, the salesman was showing someone a dark blue jacket, and Mr. Morgan was thinking of something along those lines.

Very good!

Now, listen again. Mr. Morgan is still talking to the salesman.

Salesman:	What size do you wear?
Mr. Morgan:	I take a 40 regular.
Salesman:	All the 40's are on this rack over here. This is the one the gentleman was trying on. It's 100% English wool.
Mr. Morgan:	I like the style. It's not a bad color, either. I also like this gray one here. I'd like to try both on, if I can.
Salesman:	Certainly. The mirror is over there in the corner, by the window.

Answer!

Does Mr. Morgan take a size 38 regular?	No, he doesn't take a size 38 regular.
What size does he take, a 38 regular or a 40 regular?	He takes a size 40 regular.
Did the salesman show Mr. Morgan one of the jackets?	Yes, he showed him one of the jackets.
Was it 50% English wool or 100% English wool?	It was 100% English wool.
What did Mr. Morgan think of the jacket? Did he like the style and the color?	Yes, he liked the style and the color.
Did he only look at one jacket, or did he look at another one, too?	He looked at another one, too.

Good!

Repeat!
Mr. Morgan isn't looking at jackets now.
But he was looking at jackets a few minutes ago.

The salesman isn't talking to him now. *Answer!* But he was talking ...	But he was talking to him a few minutes ago.
He isn't showing the other gentleman a jacket now. But he was ...	But he was showing him a jacket a few minutes ago.
Mr. Morgan isn't asking about jackets now. But he ...	But he was asking about jackets a few minutes ago.
He isn't trying the jacket on now. But ...	But he was trying it on a few minutes ago.

Very good!

Let's listen again. Mr Morgan is trying on the blue jacket.

    Salesman: Well, how does it feel?
Mr. Morgan: It feels a little small. Maybe I should try it in a larger size.
    Salesman: I'm sorry. We don't have that color in size 42. But we do have the gray one in that size. Would you like to try it on?
Mr. Morgan: All right.

Answer!

How does the blue jacket feel? Does it feel too big?	No, it doesn't feel too big.
It feels a little small, doesn't it?	Yes, it feels a little small.
Does Mr. Morgan want to try it on in a larger size?	Yes, he wants to try it on in a larger size.
The blue jacket feels a little small, so he wants to try it on in a larger size, right?	That's right, the blue jacket feels a little small, so he wants to try it on in a larger size.
Do they have it in size 42?	No, they don't have it in size 42.
Mr. Morgan is going to try on the gray jacket because they don't have the blue one in size 42, right?	That's right, he's going to try on the gray jacket because they don't have the blue one in size 42.

Very good! Excellent!

Let's listen again. Mr. Morgan is trying on the gray jacket.

Mr. Morgan: Ah ... this one fits much better. Yes, it's perfect. I think I'll take it!

Salesman: Will that be cash or charge?

Mr. Morgan: Charge, please.

Salesman: Fine. Oh, by the way, if you'd like to look at some shirts to go with that, there's a very good sale going on in the shirt department.

Mr. Morgan: Thanks. I'll have a look.

Answer!

Did Mr. Morgan try on the gray jacket?	Yes, he tried it on.
The gray jacket fit much better, so he's going to take it, right?	That's right, it fit much better, so he's going to take it.
How is he going to pay, by check? Or is he going to charge it?	He's going to charge it.
Has he left the store yet, or is he still talking to the salesman?	He's still talking to the salesman.
He's been talking to him for quite a while, hasn't he?	Yes, he's been talking to him for quite a while.

Very good!

Repeat!
Mr. Morgan's talking to the salesman.
He's been talking to him for quite a while.

He's looking at jackets.
Answer! He's been looking at them for ...

He's been looking at them for quite a while.

He's trying them on.
He's been trying ...

He's been trying them on for quite a while.

Macy's is having a sale.
They've been ...

They've been having a sale for quite a while.

Mr. Morgan is shopping at *Macy's*.
He's ...

He's been shopping at *Macy's* for quite a while.

Very good!

Now, let's listen to the conversation once again. This time, listen ... and repeat!

I see you're having a sale on sports jackets.

That's right. All our jackets are on sale for the next three days.
Were you looking for anything in particular?

A few minutes ago you were showing a gentleman a dark blue winter jacket.
I was thinking of something along those lines.

What size do you wear?

I take a 40 regular.

This is the one the gentleman was trying on.

I like the style. It's not a bad color, either.
I also like this gray one here.
I'd like to try both on, if I can.
It feels a little small. Maybe I should try it in a larger size.

I'm sorry. We don't have that color in size 42.
But we do have the gray one in that size.
Would you like to try it on?

Ah ... this one fits much better.
Yes, it's perfect. I think I'll take it.

Will that be cash or charge?

Charge, please.

Well, it looks like Mr. Morgan's conversation with the salesman is finished ... and our conversation, for now, is finished, too.

This is the end of Tape 6.

Tape 7   WHERE *IS* THAT WAITER?

Janet Brown is having lunch with Bob Elliott and Paula Cramer at a new restaurant that has just opened up in the area.

    Bob: Waiter, there must be some mistake. I ordered veal. I think this is chicken, isn't it?

Waiter: I'm sorry, sir, but that *is* veal.

    Bob: It sure doesn't look like veal.

Waiter: Will there be anything else?

 Paula: Not for me. ... Wait, on second thought, why don't you bring me a large glass of water?

Waiter: Yes, miss. Right away.

    Bob: I still say this tastes like chicken.

 Janet: The salad isn't the greatest, either.

 Paula: I know. It looks like it was left out overnight.

    Bob: Who recommended this place anyway? It was you, Janet, wasn't it?

 Janet: I confess. I'm the guilty one. But they just had their grand opening last week, and I thought we should give them a try.

 Paula: You mean this place is brand-new?

 Janet: Well, it's under new management. But it's been completely renovated since the new owners took over. It got a really nice write-up in last Sunday's paper.

 Paula: Where *is* that waiter with my water, anyway?

    Bob: If this is the kind of service they're going to be offering, they won't be around for long — that's for sure.

 Paula: Ah, at last! Here comes the waiter!

Waiter: Here you are, miss. You get the tomato juice, right?

Now, let's listen to the conversation once again. And then ... answer some questions.

    Bob: Waiter, there must be some mistake. I ordered veal. I think this is chicken, isn't it?

Waiter: I'm sorry, sir, but that *is* veal.

    Bob: It sure doesn't look like veal.

Waiter: Will there be anything else?

Paula: Not for me. ... Wait, on second thought, why don't you bring me a large glass of water?

Waiter: Yes, miss. Right away.

Answer!

Is Bob having lunch alone?	No, he's not having lunch alone.
I beg your pardon? Is he having lunch alone or with Janet and Paula?	He's having lunch with Janet and Paula.
Did Bob order chicken?	No, he didn't order chicken.
He ordered veal, didn't he?	Yes, he ordered veal.
Bob ordered veal, but he thinks the waiter served him chicken, right?	That's right, he ordered veal, but he thinks the waiter served him chicken.
Did he tell the waiter about it?	Yes, he told him about it.
He told him there must be some mistake, right?	That's right, he told him there must be some mistake.
What did the waiter say? Did he say it was veal?	Yes, he said it was veal.

Very good!

Now, let's listen again.

Bob: I still say this tastes like chicken.

Janet: The salad isn't the greatest, either.

Paula: I know. It looks like it was left out overnight.

Bob: Who recommended this place anyway? It was you, Janet, wasn't it?

Janet: I confess. I'm the guilty one.

Answer!

Bob thinks the veal tastes like chicken, doesn't he?	Yes, he thinks it tastes like chicken.
I'm sorry, I didn't hear you. What does Bob think about the veal?	He thinks it tastes like chicken.
The salad isn't very good either, is it?	No, it isn't very good, either.
It looks like it was left out overnight, doesn't it?	Yes, it looks like it was left out overnight.
I beg your pardon? How does it look?	It looks like it was left out overnight.

Who recommended this restaurant, Bob or Janet? — Janet recommended it.

She's the guilty one, isn't she? — Yes, she's the guilty one.

She was the one who recommended the restaurant, right? — That's right, she was the one who recommended the restaurant.

Good! Very good!

Now *you* ask the questions.

Repeat! Janet recommended the restaurant.
Question? Janet recommended the restaurant, didn't she?

Janet is the guilty one.
Question? Janet is the guilty one, isn't ... — Janet is the guilty one, isn't she?

The salad was left out overnight.
Question? The salad was ... — The salad was left out overnight, wasn't it?

Paula asked for a glass of water.
Question? Paula asked ... — Paula asked for a glass of water, didn't she?

The service is bad.
Question? The service ... — The service is bad, isn't it?

Customers have been complaining.
Question? Customers ... — Customers have been complaining, haven't they?

Very good! Excellent!

Now, listen again. Janet is still talking about the restaurant.

Janet: I confess. I'm the guilty one. But they just had their grand opening last week, and I thought we should give them a try.

Paula: You mean this place is brand-new?

Janet: Well, it's under new management. But it's been completely renovated since the new owners took over. It got a really nice write-up in last Sunday's paper.

Answer!
Is the restaurant under new management? — Yes, it's under new management.

The new owners have already taken over, haven't they? — Yes, they've already taken over.

Did the restaurant get a nice write-up in the paper? — Yes, it got a nice write-up in the paper.

It was given a really nice write-up in last Sunday's paper, right?

That's right, it was given a really nice write-up in last Sunday's paper.

The place isn't brand-new, is it?

No, it isn't brand-new.

But it has been completely renovated, hasn't it?

Yes, it's been completely renovated.

It's been completely renovated since the new owners took over, right?

That's right, it's been completely renovated since the new owners took over.

Very good!

Repeat!
They've renovated the restaurant.
The restaurant has been renovated.

They've spent a lot of money.
Answer! A lot of money has ...

A lot of money has been spent.

They've made quite a few changes.
Quite a few changes have ...

Quite a few changes have been made.

They've hired new waiters.
New waiters ...

New waiters have been hired.

They've contacted the newspaper.
The newspaper ...

The newspaper has been contacted.

They've already announced their grand opening.
Their ...

Their grand opening has already been announced.

Very good! Excellent!

Now, listen again. Paula is still waiting for a glass of water.

   Paula: Where *is* that waiter with my water, anyway?

   Bob: If this is the kind of service they're going to be offering, they won't be around for long — that's for sure.

   Paula: Ah, at last! Here comes the waiter!

   Waiter: Here you are, miss. You get the tomato juice, right?

Answer!
Was Paula waiting for a glass of water?

Yes, she was waiting for a glass of water.

Did the waiter bring it?

No, he didn't bring it.

He brought her tomato juice instead, didn't he?

Yes, he brought her tomato juice instead.

Paula asked for a glass of water, but the waiter brought her tomato juice instead, right?

That's right, she asked for a glass of water, but the waiter brought her tomato juice instead.

The service isn't very good, is it?

No, it isn't very good.

With that kind of service, they won't be around for long, right?

That's right, with that kind of service, they won't be around for long.

Very good! That was excellent!

Now, listen to the conversation once again. This time, listen ... and repeat!

Waiter, there must be some mistake. I ordered veal.
I think this is chicken, isn't it?

I'm sorry, sir, but that *is* veal.

It sure doesn't look like veal.

Will there be anything else?

Not for me.
Wait, on second thought,
why don't you bring me a large glass of water?

I still say this tastes like chicken.

The salad isn't the greatest, either.

I know. It looks like it was left out overnight.

Who recommended this place anyway?
It was *you*, Janet, wasn't it?

I confess. I'm the guilty one.
They just had their grand opening last week, and I thought we should give them a try.

Where *is* that waiter with my water, anyway?

If this is the kind of service they're going to be offering, they won't be around for long —
that's for sure.

Well, that's all the time Janet and her friends have for lunch. They're on their way back to the office now. And that's all the time we have on this tape, Tape 7.

This is the end of Tape 7.

Tape 8   WHAT'S THE TROUBLE?

One day Janet noticed Bob Elliott in the parking lot in front of the office. He seemed to be having trouble starting his car.

Janet: Hey, Bob! What's the trouble?

Bob: Oh ... Hi, Janet. I don't know what's wrong. It's a brand-new car. I've only had it a month, and now it won't start.

Janet: I know a little about cars. Would you like me to take a look?

Bob: Oh, no. I don't want you to get yourself all dirty. I'll just call the garage and have them send a tow truck.

Janet: Come on, Bob, it won't take a minute. From the sound of it, I think I know just what the problem might be.

Bob: You're kidding! ... Well, O.K., if you insist. But be careful! Don't hurt yourself ...

Janet: I won't. Hmm ... this connection doesn't look right. Turn off the ignition, Bob. And don't try starting it till I tell you.

Bob: Listen, Janet, why don't I just have the garage come out and take a look at it? I've already checked everything. There's nothing you can do.

Janet: O.K., Bob, try it now.

Bob: It started! It actually started! What did you do?

Janet: It was a loose wire right here, near the distributor.

Bob: I don't believe it! Uh ... I was just going to check that myself!

Janet: I still think you should have a mechanic look at it. You may have to have a new wire put in.

Bob: Yeah, I'll check everything out as soon as I get home. You see ... I'm used to working on older cars. With these new ones, everything's been changed around.

Janet: They *are* complicated, that's for sure.

Now, let's listen to the conversation once again. And then ... answer some questions.

Janet: Hey, Bob! What's the trouble?

Bob: Oh ... Hi, Janet. I don't know what's wrong. It's a brand-new car. I've only had it a month, and now it won't start.

Janet: I know a little about cars. Would you like me to take a look?

> Bob: Oh, no. I don't want you to get yourself all dirty. I'll just call the garage and have them send a tow truck.

Answer!

Is Bob having trouble with his motorcycle?

No, he's not having trouble with his motorcycle.

What's he having trouble with, his motorcycle or his car?

He's having trouble with his car.

It won't start, will it?

No, it won't start.

His car won't start, and Bob doesn't know what's wrong with it, right?

That's right, his car won't start, and he doesn't know what's wrong with it.

Did Janet say she knew a little about cars?

Yes, she said she knew a little about cars.

She said she knew a little about cars and she offered to help, right?

That's right, she said she knew a little about cars and she offered to help.

But Bob didn't want her to get herself all dirty, did he?

No, he didn't want her to get herself all dirty.

Does he want to call the garage?

Yes, he wants to call the garage.

He wants to have them fix his car, doesn't he?

Yes, he wants to have them fix it.

Very good!

Repeat!
He isn't going to fix the car himself.
He's going to have someone fix it.

He isn't going to check the engine himself.
Answer! He's going to have someone ...

He's going to have someone check it.

He isn't going to find the problem himself.
He's going to have ...

He's going to have someone find it.

He isn't going to work on the car himself.
He's going ...

He's going to have someone work on it.

He isn't going to tow the car himself.
He's ...
Excellent!

He's going to have someone tow it.

Listen again! Janet thinks she knows what's wrong with Bob's car.
- Bob: I'll just call the garage and have them send a tow truck.
- Janet: Come on, Bob, it won't take a minute. From the sound of it, I think I know just what the problem might be.
- Bob: You're kidding! ... Well, O.K., if you insist. But be careful! Don't hurt yourself ...
- Janet: I won't. ... Hmm ... this connection doesn't look right. Turn off the ignition, Bob. And don't try starting it till I tell you.

Answer!

Does Janet think she can fix Bob's car?	Yes, she thinks she can fix it.
Bob thought she was kidding, didn't he?	Yes, he thought she was kidding.
So, what did he do? Did he call the garage, or did he let Janet look at it?	He let her look at it.
But he told her to be careful, didn't he?	Yes, he told her to be careful.
Did Janet ask Bob to turn off the lights?	No, she didn't ask him to turn off the lights.
She asked him to turn off the ignition, didn't she?	Yes, she asked him to turn off the ignition.
Janet thought the ignition should be turned off, right?	That's right, she thought the ignition should be turned off.

Good! Very good!

Repeat!
Turn off the ignition!
The ignition should be turned off.

Check the battery. *Answer!* The battery should be ...	The battery should be checked.
Close the door. The door should ...	The door should be closed.
Put on the brake. The brake ...	The brake should be put on.
Take out the key. The key ...	The key should be taken out.

Very good!

Now, listen again. Janet is still working on Bob's car.

Bob: Listen, Janet, why don't I just have the garage come out and take a look at it? I've already checked everything. There's nothing you can do.

Janet: O.K., Bob, try it now.

Bob: It started! It actually started! What did you do?

Janet: It was a loose wire right here, near the distributor.

Bob: I don't believe it! Uh ... I was just going to check that myself!

Answer!

Did Bob's car actually start?	Yes, it actually started.
Did Bob get it started?	No, he didn't get it started.
Janet got it started, didn't she?	Yes, Janet got it started.
She found a loose wire near the distributor, didn't she?	Yes, she found a loose wire near the distributor.
She found a loose wire near the distributor, and that's how she got the car started, right?	That's right, she found a loose wire near the distributor, and that's how she got the car started.

Good!

Now let's listen to the rest of the conversation.

Janet: I still think you should have a mechanic look at it. You may have to have a new wire put in.

Bob: Yeah, I'll check everything out as soon as I get home. You see ... I'm used to working on older cars. With these new ones, everything's been changed around.

Janet: They *are* complicated, that's for sure.

Answer!

Does Janet think the problem is over?	No, she doesn't think it's over.
She still thinks Bob should have a mechanic look at his car, doesn't she?	Yes, she still thinks he should have a mechanic look at it.
Why? Because he may have to have a new wire put in?	Yes, because he may have to have a new wire put in.
Is Bob going to check out the problem now?	No, he's not going to check it out now.
He'll check it out when he gets home, won't he?	Yes, he'll check it out when he gets home.
He's not used to working on new cars, is he?	No, he's not used to working on new cars.

They're complicated, and he's not used to working on them, right?	That's right, they're complicated, and he's not used to working on them.

Very good! Excellent!

Now, listen to the conversation once again. This time, listen ... and repeat!

Hey, Bob! What's the trouble?

I don't know what's wrong. It's a brand-new car.
I've only had it a month, and now it won't start.

I know a little about cars. Would you like me to take a look?

Oh, no. I don't want you to get yourself all dirty.
I'll just call the garage and have them send a tow truck.

Come on, Bob, it won't take a minute.
From the sound of it, I think I know just what the problem might be.

You're kidding!
Well, O.K., if you insist. But be careful! Don't hurt yourself.

O.K., Bob, try it now.

It started! It actually started! What did you do?

It was a loose wire right here, near the distributor.

I don't believe it!
I was just going to check that myself!

I still think you should have a mechanic look at it.

Yeah, I'll check everything out as soon as I get home.

Well, Janet helped Bob get his car started, so he's on his way. And we have to be on our way, too. That's all the time we have for this tape, Tape 8.

This is the end of Tape 8.

Tape 9   YOU REALLY HAD QUITE A DAY!

Janet was on her way home from work one day when she ran into her friend Bill Sinclair.

Janet: Bill! Where did you get that black eye? And what are you doing here anyway? I thought you had already left for Vermont. When I saw you at work yesterday, you said you had already packed and were all set to go.

Bill: It's a long story. You see, the whole reason for my vacation was to get away and relax a little. I was even going to take the train, so I could enjoy the scenery on the way up. The trouble started this morning when my alarm clock didn't go off. By the time I got to the station, my train had already left. The next train wasn't due to leave for 12 hours, so I decided to rent a car instead.

Janet: That sounds like a good idea.

Bill: That's what *I* thought! But on my way to the car rental agency, I slipped and fell down some stairs in the subway.

Janet: So *that's* how you got the black eye!

Bill: I'm lucky I didn't kill myself! Anyway, when I fell, I broke my glasses and had to go all the way back home to pick up my other pair.

Janet: You really had quite a day!

Bill: And if you think it was easy lugging these suitcases all over town ... Anyway, when I finally got to the rental agency, the place was packed. After I had waited in line for half an hour and filled out all the forms, I realized I couldn't pay. It turned out I had left my wallet at home.

Janet: You sure have been through a lot! So what are you going to do now?

Bill: Well, for one thing, I've decided to forget about going to Vermont. I'm already a physical wreck, and I haven't even left town yet!

Now let's listen to the conversation once again. And then ... answer some questions.

Janet: Bill! Where did you get that black eye? And what are you doing here anyway? I thought you had already left for Vermont. When I saw you at work yesterday, you said you had already packed and were all set to go.

Bill: It's a long story. You see, the whole reason for my vacation was to get away and relax a little. I was even going to take the train, so I could enjoy the scenery on the way up.

Answer!

Did Bill have a black eye?
Yes, he had a black eye.

Had he already left for Vermont?
No, he hadn't left for Vermont yet.

But he had already packed his bags, hadn't he?
Yes, he had already packed his bags.

He had already packed his bags when he left work the day before, right?
That's right, he had already packed his bags when he left work the day before.

The reason for his vacation was to get away and relax a little, right?

That's right, the reason for his vacation was to get away and relax a little.

Was he going to take a plane or a train to Vermont?

He was going to take a train to Vermont.

He was going to take a train so he could enjoy the scenery, right?

That's right, he was going to take a train so he could enjoy the scenery.

Very good!

Listen again. Bill's telling Janet what went wrong with his vacation plans.

    Bill: The trouble started this morning when my alarm clock didn't go off. By the time I got to the station, my train had already left. The next train wasn't due to leave for 12 hours, so I decided to rent a car instead.

    Janet: That sounds like a good idea.

    Bill: That's what *I* thought! But on my way to the car rental agency, I slipped and fell down some stairs in the subway.

Answer!
Did Bill have an accident?

Yes, he had an accident.

What happened? Did he slip and fall down some stairs?

Yes, he slipped and fell down some stairs.

Did he catch his train when he got to the station?

No, he didn't catch his train when he got to the station.

What happened? Had the train already left when he got to the station?

Yes, it had already left when he got to the station.

What did he decide to do, wait for the next train or rent a car?

He decided to rent a car.

Very good! Excellent!

Repeat!
The train left.
When he got to the station, the train had already left.

He packed his bags.
When he got to the station, he had already packed his bags.

He ate breakfast.
Answer! When he got to the station, he had already ...

When he got to the station, he had already eaten breakfast.

He had two cups of coffee. When he got to the station ...	When he got to the station, he had already had two cups of coffee.
He planned the whole trip. When he ...	When he got to the station, he had already planned the whole trip.
He paid for his ticket. When ...	When he got to the station, he had already paid for his ticket.

Very good!

Listen again!

>*Bill:* I slipped and fell down some stairs in the subway.
>
>*Janet:* So *that's* how you got the black eye!
>
>*Bill:* I'm lucky I didn't kill myself! Anyway, when I fell, I broke my glasses and had to go all the way back home to pick up my other pair.
>
>*Janet:* You really had quite a day!
>
>*Bill:* And if you think it was easy lugging these suitcases all over town ...

Answer!

Bill got a black eye when he fell down some stairs, didn't he?	Yes, he got a black eye when he fell down some stairs.
Did he break his glasses or his watch?	He broke his glasses.
Ah, when Bill fell down, he got a black eye and broke his glasses too, right?	That's right, when he fell down, he got a black eye and broke his glasses, too.
He's lucky he didn't kill himself, isn't he?	Yes, he's lucky he didn't kill himself.

Good! Very good!

Now let's listen to the rest of Bill's conversation with Janet.

>*Bill:* Anyway, when I finally got to the rental agency, the place was packed. After I had waited in line for half an hour and filled out all the forms, I realized I couldn't pay. It turned out I had left my wallet at home.
>
>*Janet:* You sure have been through a lot! So what are you going to do now?
>
>*Bill:* Well, for one thing, I've decided to forget about going to Vermont. I'm already a physical wreck, and I haven't even left town yet!

Answer!

Did Bill finally get to the car rental agency?	Yes, he finally got to the car rental agency.
Could he pay for the car?	No, he couldn't pay for it.

Why not? Had he left his wallet at home?

Yes, he had left his wallet at home.

He had left his wallet at home, so he couldn't pay for the car, right?

That's right, he had left his wallet at home, so he couldn't pay for the car.

He sure has been through a lot, hasn't he?

Yes, he sure has been through a lot.

He didn't even leave town, did he?

No, he didn't even leave town.

When he saw Janet, he hadn't even left town yet, right?

That's right, when he saw Janet, he hadn't even left town yet.

Good! Very good!

Repeat!
He didn't leave town.
When he saw Janet, he hadn't left town yet.

He didn't go to Vermont.
Answer! When he saw Janet, he hadn't gone ...

When he saw Janet, he hadn't gone to Vermont yet.

He didn't rent a car.
When he saw Janet, he hadn't ...

When he saw Janet, he hadn't rented a car yet.

He didn't unpack his bags.
When he saw ...

When he saw Janet, he hadn't unpacked his bags yet.

He didn't take his vacation.
When he ...

When he saw Janet, he hadn't taken his vacation yet.

Very good! That was excellent!

Now, listen to the conversation once again. This time, listen ... and repeat!

Bill! Where did you get that black eye?
And what are you doing here anyway?
I thought you had already left for Vermont.

It's a long story.
You see, the whole reason for my vacation was to get away and relax a little.
I was even going to take the train
so I could enjoy the scenery on the way up.
By the time I got to the station, my train had already left.
So I decided to rent a car instead.

That sounds like a good idea.

That's what *I* thought!

But on my way to the car rental agency, I slipped and fell down some stairs in the subway.

So *that's* how you got the black eye!

I'm lucky I didn't kill myself!

You sure have been through a lot! So what are you going to do now?

Well, for one thing, I've decided to forget about going to Vermont.

I'm already a physical wreck, and I haven't even left town yet!

Well, it looks like Bill's vacation is over before it even started. And this tape, Tape 9, is over, too.

This is the end of Tape 9.

Tape 10   AN INVITATION

Susan Morgan and her husband, John, are relaxing in their living room after dinner.

Susan: Oh, John, I forgot to tell you — Linda Stamford called a couple of days ago. She said Ed had just gotten a big promotion.

John: But he hasn't been with that company very long, has he? Didn't he just start there about six months ago?

Susan: That's right. Apparently, it all started about a month ago when Ed got a terrific job offer from a company in Texas. Linda said he'd almost decided to accept the job when his company heard about the offer and gave him a big promotion ... with a much higher salary! They even promised him a company car as part of the deal.

John: So what did he decide to do?

Susan: He decided to stay where he is. Now he wants to throw a party to celebrate, and Linda called to invite us. She told me she'd already invited about twenty people.

John: When is it?

Susan: This Saturday night.

John: Hmm ... they're not giving us much notice. And didn't you tell me last week that you'd gotten theater tickets for Saturday night?

Susan: Oh, that's right! I'd forgotten all about it. Well ... what do you think we should do, go to the party or see the play?

John: I'd rather go to the party. Why don't we give the theater tickets to the Randalls?

Susan: We can't. They've been invited to the party, too!

John: I know. I'll give them to my secretary, Janet. I think she has a new boyfriend.

Now, let's listen to the conversation once again. And then ... answer some questions.

Susan: Oh, John, I forgot to tell you — Linda Stamford called a couple of days ago. She said Ed had just gotten a big promotion.

John: But he hasn't been with that company very long, has he? Didn't he just start there about six months ago?

Susan: That's right.

Answer!

Has Ed Stamford been with his company for a long time?	No, he hasn't been with his company for a long time.
He just started working there about six months ago, didn't he?	Yes, he just started working there about six months ago.
Who called Susan Morgan a couple of days ago? Was it Ed or his wife, Linda?	It was his wife, Linda.
Did Linda say her husband had gotten a transfer?	No, she didn't say he'd gotten a transfer.
She said he had gotten a promotion, right?	That's right, she said he had gotten a promotion.

Very good!

Repeat!
He got a promotion.
Linda said he had gotten a promotion.

He got a raise, too.
Answer! Linda said he had gotten ...
Linda said he had gotten a raise, too.

He received a good offer.
She said he had ...
She said he had received a good offer.

He thought it over carefully.
She said he ...
She said he had thought it over carefully.

He decided to stay with his company.
She said ...
She said he had decided to stay with his company.

Tape Ten (cont'd.)

He hasn't been with his company very long.
She said ...

She said he hadn't been with his company very long.

Good! Very good!

Now listen again. Mrs. Morgan is telling her husband more about Ed's promotion.

Susan: Apparently, it all started about a month ago when Ed got a terrific job offer from a company in Texas. Linda said he'd almost decided to accept the job when his company heard about the offer and gave him a big promotion ... with a much higher salary! They even promised him a company car as part of the deal.

John: So what did he decide to do?

Susan: He decided to stay where he is.

Answer!

Did Ed get a terrific job offer?

Yes, he got a terrific job offer.

Linda said he had almost decided to accept the offer, didn't she?

Yes, she said he had almost decided to accept the offer.

She said he had gotten a terrific job offer and had almost decided to accept it, right?

That's right, she said he had gotten a terrific job offer and had almost decided to accept it.

What happened then? What did Ed's company do? Did they decide to let him go?

No, they didn't decide to let him go.

They gave him a big promotion, right?

That's right, they gave him a big promotion.

So what did Ed do? Did he decide to go to Texas or stay where he is?

He decided to stay where he is.

Very good! Excellent!

Let's listen again.

Susan: He decided to stay where he is. Now he wants to throw a party to celebrate, and Linda called to invite us. She told me she'd already invited about twenty people.

John: When is it?

Susan: This Saturday night.

John: Hmm ... they're not giving us much notice. And didn't you tell me last week that you'd gotten theater tickets for Saturday night?

Susan: Oh, that's right! I'd forgotten all about it.

Answer!

What does Ed have in mind? Does he want to go on a vacation or throw a party?	He wants to throw a party.
He wants to throw a party to celebrate his big promotion, right?	That's right, he wants to throw a party to celebrate his big promotion.
Did Linda invite the Morgans to the party?	Yes, she invited them to the party.
Did she say the party was going to be this Friday or this Saturday night?	She said it was going to be this Saturday night.
But Mrs. Morgan had already gotten theater tickets for Saturday night, hadn't she?	Yes, she had already gotten theater tickets for Saturday night.
Did Mr. Morgan ask her if she had gotten the tickets?	Yes, he asked her if she had gotten them.

Very good!

Repeat!

Did you get the tickets? He asked her if she had gotten the tickets.	
Did you pay for them? He asked her if she had ...	He asked her if she had paid for them.
Did you speak to Linda? He asked her if she ...	He asked her if she had spoken to Linda.
What did she say? He asked her what ...	He asked her what she had said.
Did Linda invite us? He asked her ...	He asked her if Linda had invited them.
What time did she call? He asked ...	He asked her what time she had called.

Very good! Excellent!

Now, let's listen to the rest of the conversation.

Susan: Well ... what do you think we should do, go to the party or see the play?

John: I'd rather go to the party. Why don't we give the theater tickets to the Randalls?

Susan: We can't. They've been invited to the party, too!

> John: I know. I'll give them to my secretary, Janet. I think she has a new boyfriend.

Answer!

Did the Morgans decide to go to the play?	No, they didn't decide to go to the play.
John told Susan he'd rather go to the party, didn't he?	Yes, he told her he'd rather go to the party.
Are they going to give their theater tickets to the Randalls?	No, they aren't going to give them to the Randalls.
They can't give their tickets to the Randalls because the Randalls have been invited to the party, too, right?	That's right, they can't give their tickets to the Randalls because the Randalls have been invited to the party, too.
But Mr. Morgan isn't going to throw the tickets away, is he?	No, he isn't going to throw them away.
I beg your pardon? Is he going to throw the tickets away or give them to his secretary, Janet?	He's going to give them to his secretary, Janet.

Good!

Now, let's listen to the conversation once again. This time, listen ... and repeat!

Oh, John, I forgot to tell you —
Linda Stamford called a couple of days ago.
She said Ed had just gotten a big promotion.

But he hasn't been with that company very long, has he?
Didn't he just start there about six months ago?

Apparently, it all started when Ed got a terrific job offer from a company in Texas.
His company heard about the offer
and gave him a big promotion ... with a much higher salary!
They even promised him a company car as part of the deal.

So what did he decide to do?

He decided to stay where he is.
Now he wants to throw a party to celebrate.
Linda called to invite us.

Didn't you tell me last week that you'd gotten theater tickets for Saturday night?

Oh, that's right! I'd forgotten all about it.
Well ... what do you think we should do, go to the party or see the play?

I'd rather go to the party.

Well, it looks like Mr. and Mrs. Morgan will be going to the party after all ... and we have to be going now, too. Their fun is about to begin, but this tape, Tape 10, is about to end.

This is the end of Tape 10.

Tape 11   CONGRATULATIONS!

Kevin Williams, manager of Superior Products' London office, is meeting with John Morgan in New York.

John: So, Kevin, that's the situation. After three years of trying to establish a foothold in Europe, the results are still disappointing. To tell you the truth, we've actually considered closing down the European operation altogether.

Kevin: Closing down? I didn't realize the situation was *that* serious. In London, we've been rather optimistic.

John: I can understand that. Your office is the only one that's shown an increase in sales ... and profits.

Kevin: Yes, but remember — it took us three years to do it. If I were you, John, I would give the other managers a little more time. I'm sure they can show positive results, too.

John: I'm not so sure, Kevin. Look ... we've invested an enormous amount of money in these operations, and we don't have much to show for it. But in your case, we've seen steady results right from the start.

Kevin: Well, we *have* been quite successful so far. I'm not really that familiar with the other operations. Each country is really quite different. Each one has its own set of problems.

John: But they all need one thing — energetic leadership. That's been the key to *your* success. I'm convinced of it! I'm not sure the other managers are as much on top of their operations as they could be.

Kevin: Well, I suppose that's possible, but ...

John: No "but's" about it. We have a problem. But we may also have a solution. Kevin, I need someone who can take charge of the entire European operation — someone with a lot of experience, and someone with a successful track record. How does the title *Vice President — European Operations* sound to you?

Kevin: Vice President?

Tape Eleven (cont'd.)

John: You've earned it, Kevin. Congratulations!

Kevin: Thanks, John. I hope I won't disappoint you.

Now, let's listen to the conversation once again ... and then answer some questions.

John: So, Kevin, that's the situation. After three years of trying to establish a foothold in Europe, the results are still disappointing. To tell you the truth, we've actually considered closing down the European operation altogether.

Kevin: Closing down? I didn't realize the situation was *that* serious.

Answer!

Has John been trying to establish a foothold in Europe?	Yes, he's been trying to establish a foothold in Europe.
I'm sorry, I didn't hear you. Where has he been trying to establish a foothold?	He's been trying to establish a foothold in Europe.
John has been trying to establish a foothold in Europe for three years, but the results are still disappointing, right?	That's right, he's been trying to establish a foothold in Europe for three years, but the results are still disappointing.
He's even considered closing down the European operation, hasn't he?	Yes, he's even considered closing down the European operation.
Did Kevin know about that?	No, he didn't know about that.
He didn't realize the situation was that serious, did he?	No, he didn't realize the situation was that serious.

Good!

Let's listen again.

Kevin: I didn't realize the situation was *that* serious. In London, we've been rather optimistic.

John: I can understand that. Your office is the only one that's shown an increase in sales ... and profits.

Kevin: Yes, but remember — it took us three years to do it. If I were you, John, I would give the other managers a little more time. I'm sure they can show positive results, too.

John: I'm not so sure, Kevin.

Answer!

Does John's company have a serious problem in Europe?	Yes, it has a serious problem in Europe.

Business hasn't been good, has it?	No, it hasn't been good.
But the London office has shown an increase in sales, hasn't it?	Yes, the London office has shown an increase in sales.
Does Kevin think the other managers can show positive results, too?	Yes, he thinks they can show positive results, too.
But he thinks they'll need more time, doesn't he?	Yes, he thinks they'll need more time.
If he were John, he would give them more time, right?	That's right, if he were John, he would give them more time.

Very good!

Repeat!
You should give them more time.
If I were you, I would give them more time.

You shouldn't rush them.
Answer! If I were you, I wouldn't ...   If I were you, I wouldn't rush them.

You should invest more money.
If I were you, I would ...   If I were you, I would invest more money.

You shouldn't close down the operation.
If I were you ...   If I were you, I wouldn't close down the operation.

You should improve the advertising.
If I ...   If I were you, I would improve the advertising.

Very good! That was excellent!

Let's listen again. John's explaining the problem.

> John: Look ... we've invested an enormous amount of money in these operations, and we don't have much to show for it. But in your case, we've seen steady results right from the start.
>
> Kevin: Well, we *have* been quite successful so far. I'm not really that familiar with the other operations. Each country is really quite different. Each one has its own set of problems.
>
> John: But they all need one thing — energetic leadership. That's been the key to *your* success. I'm convinced of it!

Answer!

The European managers aren't doing well, are they?	No, they aren't doing well.

Tape Eleven (cont'd.)

What about Kevin? Has his office been successful?	Yes, his office has been successful.
Energetic leadership — Is that the key to Kevin's success?	Yes, that's the key to his success.
John's convinced that energetic leadership has been the key to Kevin's success, right?	That's right, John's convinced that energetic leadership has been the key to Kevin's success.
Very good!	

Repeat!
We have to have good leadership.
It's important for us to have good leadership.

We have to take charge of things. *Answer!* It's important for us to ...	It's important for us to take charge of things.
We have to train the managers. It's important for us ...	It's important for us to train the managers.
They have to show positive results. It's important for ...	It's important for them to show positive results.
They have to understand the situation. It's important ...	It's important for them to understand the situation.
They have to improve sales. It's ...	It's important for them to improve sales.

Very good! Excellent!

Now, let's listen again.

John: I'm not sure the other managers are as much on top of their operations as they could be.

Kevin: Well, I suppose that's possible, but ...

John: No "but's" about it. We have a problem. But we may also have a solution. Kevin, I need someone who can take charge of the entire European operation — someone with a lot of experience, and someone with a successful track record. How does the title *Vice President — European Operations* sound to you?

Kevin: Vice President?

John: You've earned it, Kevin. Congratulations!

Kevin: Thanks, John. I hope I won't disappoint you.

Answer!

Does John need someone to take charge of the European operation?

Yes, he needs someone to take charge of the European operation.

He needs someone with a successful track record and a lot of experience, right?

That's right, he needs someone with a successful track record and a lot of experience.

Who does he have in mind for the job, himself or Kevin?

He has Kevin in mind.

Very good!

Now, listen to the conversation once again. This time, listen ... and repeat!

So, Kevin, that's the situation.
To tell you the truth, we've actually considered closing down the European operation altogether.

Closing down? I didn't realize the situation was *that* serious.
In London, we've been rather optimistic.

Your office is the only one that's shown an increase in sales ... and profits.

If I were you, John, I would give the other managers a little more time.
I'm sure they can show positive results, too.

I'm not so sure, Kevin.
But they all need one thing — energetic leadership.
That's been the key to *your* success. I'm convinced of it!
I need someone with a lot of experience
and someone with a successful track record.
How does the title *Vice President — European Operations* sound to you?
You've earned it, Kevin. Congratulations!

Thanks, John. I hope I won't disappoint you.

Well, it looks like Kevin will be moving on to a new assignment. And *we* have to be moving on, too ... because this tape, Tape 11, is almost over.

This is the end of Tape 11.

Tape 12   I WON'T BE A MINUTE

Kevin Williams and his wife, Sarah, have ended their stay in New York and are returning to London. Right now, they're at the airline ticket counter at JFK Airport in New York.

... Trans National Airlines Flight 915 to Rome is now boarding at Gate 22. All passengers please proceed to Gate 22.

Attendant: Yes ... may I help you?

Kevin: We'd like to check in for Flight 807 to London.

Attendant: May I see your tickets and passports, please? ... Thank you. How many bags do you have?

Kevin: Three suitcases, plus these two flight bags. It's a good thing we bought the second flight bag, Sarah. If we didn't have it, there wouldn't be enough room for all the presents and souvenirs.

Sarah: We *did* get a lot, didn't we?

Kevin: Oh, well, we picked up some really nice things, and some good bargains, too.

Attendant: Would you prefer a smoking or non-smoking section?

Kevin: Non-smoking, please. Oh, and we'd like a window seat, if possible.

Attendant: Certainly. Here are your boarding passes and your baggage claim tickets. Your flight will be boarding in about 30 minutes.

Kevin: Thank you. ... Well, what shall we do now? I'm rather hungry myself.

Sarah: I am, too. We haven't had a bite to eat since lunch.

Kevin: Hmm ... if our flight weren't leaving so soon, we could have a snack in that restaurant over there. Oh, well, it doesn't matter. We'll be having dinner on the plane in a little while anyway.

Sarah: You're right. But I would like to get something to read. Do you think there's time for me to run back to the newsstand and get a magazine?

Kevin: I think so. But I wouldn't take too long if I were you. Remember, the next flight doesn't leave till tomorrow afternoon!

Sarah: Don't worry. I won't be a minute. I'm not too anxious to spend the night here at the airport!

Now, let's listen to the conversation once again. And then ... answer some questions.

... Trans National Airlines Flight 915 to Rome is now boarding at Gate 22. All passengers please proceed to Gate 22.

Attendant: Yes ... may I help you?

Kevin: We'd like to check in for Flight 807 to London.

Attendant: May I see your tickets and passports, please? ... Thank you. How many bags do you have?

Kevin: Three suitcases, plus these two flight bags.

Answer!

Are Kevin and Sarah checking in for a flight to Rome?	No, they're not checking in for a flight to Rome.
They're checking in for Flight 807 to London, aren't they?	Yes, they're checking in for Flight 807 to London.
Do they have five suitcases?	No, they don't have five suitcases.
They have three suitcases plus two flight bags, right?	That's right, they have three suitcases plus two flight bags.
If the Williams didn't have their tickets, they couldn't check in, could they?	No, if they didn't have their tickets, they couldn't check in.

Very good!

Repeat!
They can check in.
If they didn't have their tickets, they couldn't check in.

They can go through the gate.
Answer!

If they didn't have their tickets, they couldn't go ...	If they didn't have their tickets, they couldn't go through the gate.
They can get on the plane. If they didn't have their tickets ...	If they didn't have their tickets, they couldn't get on the plane.
They can leave New York. If they didn't have ...	If they didn't have their tickets, they couldn't leave New York.
They can return to London. If they ...	If they didn't have their tickets, they couldn't return to London.

Good!

Let's listen again. Kevin and Sarah are still at the airline ticket counter.

Kevin: It's a good thing we bought the second flight bag, Sarah. If we didn't have it, there wouldn't be enough room for all the presents and souvenirs.

Sarah: We *did* get a lot, didn't we?

Kevin: Oh, well, we picked up some really nice things, and some good bargains, too.

Attendant: Would you prefer a smoking or non-smoking section?

Tape Twelve (cont'd.)

Kevin: Non-smoking, please. Oh, and we'd like a window seat, if possible.

Attendant: Certainly.

Answer!

Did the Williams buy a lot of souvenirs while they were in New York?	Yes, they bought a lot of souvenirs while they were in New York.
Was everything in New York very expensive, or did they get some good bargains?	They got some good bargains.
Do they have enough room for everything they bought?	Yes, they have enough room for everything they bought.
If they didn't have the second flight bag, they wouldn't have enough room, would they?	No, if they didn't have the second flight bag, they wouldn't have enough room.
Do Kevin and Sarah want to sit in the smoking section?	No, they don't want to sit in the smoking section.
If possible, they'd like a window seat in the non-smoking section, right?	That's right, if possible, they'd like a window seat in the non-smoking section.

Good!

Let's listen again.

Attendant: Here are your boarding passes and your baggage claim tickets. Your flight will be boarding in about 30 minutes.

Kevin: Thank you. ... Well, what shall we do now? I'm rather hungry myself.

Sarah: I am, too. We haven't had a bite to eat since lunch.

Kevin: Hmm ... if our flight weren't leaving so soon, we could have a snack in that restaurant over there. Oh, well, it doesn't matter. We'll be having dinner on the plane in a little while anyway.

Sarah: You're right. But I would like to get something to read.

Answer!

Have Kevin and Sarah had anything to eat?	No, they haven't had anything to eat.
Do they have time to get a snack?	No, they don't have time to get a snack.
Why not? Is their flight leaving soon?	Yes, it's leaving soon.

Their flight is leaving soon, so they don't have time to get a snack, right?

That's right, their flight is leaving soon, so they don't have time to get a snack.

But if they had more time, they would get a snack, wouldn't they?

Yes, if they had more time, they would get a snack.

Very good!

Repeat!
They're not going to get a snack.
If they had more time, they would get a snack.

They're not going to buy more souvenirs.
Answer! If they had more time, they would buy ...

If they had more time, they would buy more souvenirs.

They're not going to make a phone call.
If they had more time, they would ...

If they had more time, they would make a phone call.

They're not going to take a walk.
If they had more time ...

If they had more time, they would take a walk.

They're not going to stay in New York.
If ...

If they had more time, they would stay in New York.

Very good! Excellent!

Now, let's listen to the rest of the conversation.

 Sarah: I would like to get something to read. Do you think there's time for me to run back to the newsstand and get a magazine?

 Kevin: I think so. But I wouldn't take too long if I were you. Remember, the next flight doesn't leave till tomorrow afternoon!

 Sarah: Don't worry. I won't be a minute. I'm not too anxious to spend the night here at the airport!

Answer!
Who's going to the newsstand, Kevin or Sarah?

Sarah's going to the newsstand.

Did Kevin tell her not to take too long?

Yes, he told her not to take too long.

Is there another flight today?

No, there isn't another flight today.

The next flight doesn't leave till tomorrow afternoon, right?

That's right, the next flight doesn't leave till tomorrow afternoon.

Sarah's not very anxious to spend the night at the airport, is she?

No, she's not very anxious to spend the night at the airport.

Very good!

Now, let's listen to the conversation once again. This time, listen ... and repeat!

Yes, may I help you?

We'd like to check in for Flight 807 to London.

May I see your tickets and passports, please?
Thank you. How many bags do you have?

Three suitcases, plus these two flight bags.

Would you prefer a smoking or non-smoking section?

Non-smoking, please.
Oh, and we'd like a window seat, if possible.

Certainly.
Here are your boarding passes and your baggage claim tickets.
Your flight will be boarding in about 30 minutes.

If our flight weren't leaving so soon, we could have a snack in that restaurant over there.

Oh, well, it doesn't matter.

Do you think there's time for me to run back to the newsstand and get a magazine?

I think so. But I wouldn't take too long if I were you.

Well, it looks like the Williams' stay in New York is just about over. And this tape, Tape 12, is just about over, too.

This is the end of Tape 12 ... and it's also the end of this program. We hope the program has helped you to understand more ... to speak better ... to *Brush Up Your English*.